Interactive Math Notebook: Grade 7

Authors: Schyrlet Cameron and Carolyn Craig

Editor: Mary Dieterich

Proofreaders: Alexis Fey and Margaret Brown

COPYRIGHT © 2020 Mark Twain Media, Inc.

ISBN 978-1-62223-814-9

Printing No. CD-405046

Mark Twain Media, Inc., Publishers
Distributed by Carson-Dellosa Publishing LLC

Visit us at www.carsondellosa.com

Table of Contents

Introduction

The *Interactive Math Notebook: Grade 7* is designed to allow students to become active participants in their own learning. The book lays out an easy-to-follow plan for setting up, creating, and maintaining an interactive notebook.

An interactive notebook is simply a spiral notebook that students use to store and organize important information. It is a culmination of student work throughout the unit of study. Once completed, the notebook becomes the student's own personalized notebook and a great resource for reviewing and studying for tests.

The intent of the book is to help students make sense of new information. Textbooks often present more facts and data than students can process at one time. This book introduces each concept in an easy-to-read and easy-to-understand format that does not overwhelm the learner. The text presents only the most important information, making it easier for students to comprehend. Vocabulary words are printed in boldfaced type.

The book focuses on the critical areas for mathematics in grade seven. The 28 lessons cover 5 units of study: The Number System, Ratios and Proportional Relationships, Expressions and Equations, Geometry, and Statistics and Probability. The units can be used in the order presented or in an order that best fits the classroom curriculum. Teachers can easily differentiate units to address the individual learning levels and needs of students. The lessons are designed to support state and national standards. Each lesson consists of two pages that are used to create the right-hand and left-hand pages of the interactive notebook.

- **Input page:** essential information for understanding the lesson concepts and directions for creating the interactive page.
- **Output page:** hands-on activity such as a foldable or graphic organizer to help students process essential information from the lesson.

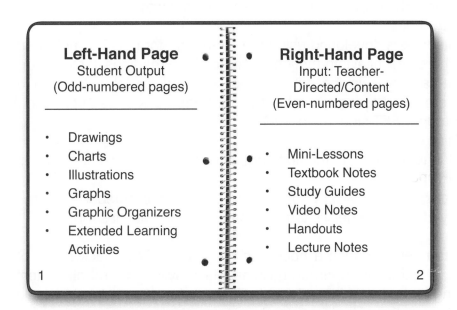

Left-Hand Page
Student Output
(Odd-numbered pages)
_____

- Drawings
- Charts
- Illustrations
- Graphs
- Graphic Organizers
- Extended Learning Activities

1

Right-Hand Page
Input: Teacher-
Directed/Content
(Even-numbered pages)
_____

- Mini-Lessons
- Textbook Notes
- Study Guides
- Video Notes
- Handouts
- Lecture Notes

2

Organizing an Interactive Notebook

What Is an Interactive Notebook?

Does this sound familiar? "I can't find my homework…class notes…study guide." If so, the interactive notebook is a tool you can use to help manage this problem. An interactive notebook is simply a notebook that students use to record, store, and organize their work. The "interactive" aspect of the notebook comes from the fact that students are working with information in various ways as they fill in the notebook. Once completed, the notebook becomes the student's own personalized study guide and a great resource for reviewing information, reinforcing concepts, and studying for tests.

Materials Needed to Create an Interactive Notebook

- Notebook (spiral, composition, or binder with loose-leaf paper)
- Glue stick
- Scissors
- Colored pencils (we do not recommend using markers)
- Tabs

Creating an Interactive Notebook

A good time to introduce the interactive notebook is at the beginning of a new unit of study. Use the following steps to get started.

Step 1: *Notebook Cover*

Students design a cover to reflect the units of study. They should add their names and other important information as directed by the teacher.

Step 2: *Grading Rubric*

Take time to discuss the grading rubric with the students. It is important for each student to understand the expectations for creating the interactive notebook.

Step 3: *Table of Contents*

Students label the first several pages of the notebook "Table of Contents." When completing a new page, they add its title to the table of contents.

Step 4: *Creating Pages*

The notebook is developed using the dual-page format. The right-hand side is the input page where essential information and notes from readings, lectures, or videos are placed. The left-hand side is the output page reserved for foldable activities, charts, graphic organizers, etc. Students number the front and back of each page in the bottom outside corner (odd: LEFT-side; even: RIGHT-side).

Step 5: *Tab Units*

Add a tab to the edge of the first page of each unit to make it easy to flip to the unit.

Step 6: *Glossary*

Students reserve several pages at the back of the notebook where they can create a glossary of domain-specific terms encountered in each lesson.

Step 7: *Pocket*

Students need to attach a pocket to the inside of the back cover of the notebook for storage of handouts, returned quizzes, class syllabus, and other items that don't seem to belong on pages of the notebook. This can be an envelope, resealable plastic bag, or students can design their own pocket.

Left-hand and Right-hand Notebook Pages

Interactive notebooks are usually viewed open like a textbook. This allows the student to view the left-hand page and right-hand page at the same time. Traditionally, the right-hand page is used as the input or the content part of the lesson. The left-hand page is the student output part of the lesson. This is where the students have an opportunity to show what they have learned in a creative and colorful way. (Color helps the brain remember information.)

The format of the interactive notebook involves both the right-brain and left-brain hemispheres to help students

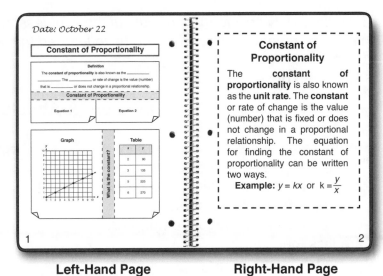

Left-Hand Page   Right-Hand Page

process information. When creating the pages, start with the left-hand page. First, have students date the page. Students then move to the right-hand page and the teacher-directed part of the lesson. Finally, students use the information they have learned to complete the left-hand page. Above is an example of completed right- and left-hand pages.

Interactive Notebook Grading Rubric

Interactive Math Notebook: Grade 7, Grading Rubric				
Category	**4**	**3**	**2**	**1**
Table of Contents	Table of contents is complete.	Table of contents is mostly complete.	Table of contents is somewhat complete.	Attempt was made to include table of contents.
Organization	All pages in correct order. All are numbered, dated, and titled correctly.	Most pages in correct order. Most are numbered, dated, and titled correctly.	Some pages in correct order. Some are numbered, dated, and titled correctly.	Few pages in correct order. Few are numbered, dated, and titled correctly.
Content	All information complete, accurate, and placed in the correct order. All spelling correct.	Most information complete, accurate, and placed in the correct order. Most spelling correct.	Some information complete, accurate, and placed in the correct order. Some spelling errors.	Few pages correctly completed. Many spelling errors.
Appearance	All notebook pages are neat and colorful.	Most notebook pages are neat and colorful.	Some notebook pages are neat and colorful.	Few notebook pages are neat and colorful.
Teacher's Comments:				

Student Instructions: Integers & Absolute Value

Read the following information. Cut out the mini-lesson and attach it to the right-hand page of your interactive notebook. Use what you have learned to create the left-hand page.

Mini-Lesson

Integers & Absolute Value

Integers are the set of whole numbers and their opposites. The set includes positive numbers, negative numbers, and zero. **Positive numbers** are greater than zero. **Negative numbers** are less than zero.

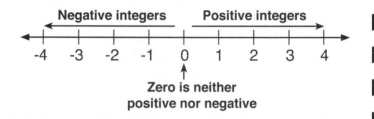

Zero is neither positive nor negative

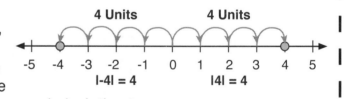

Opposites are a pair of numbers that are equal distances from zero on opposite sides of zero.

Symbols (<, >, or =) are used to show the relationship between positive and negative numbers.

Symbol	Meaning	Example
<	is less than	-3 < 5
>	is greater than	-2 > -4
=	is equal to	-1 = -1

Absolute value of a number can be considered as the distance between the number and zero on a number line. Since distance cannot be negative, the absolute value of every number will be either positive or zero. **Absolute value means to remove any negative sign in front of a number.** Vertical bars, | |, are used to show absolute value.

Example:
The integers -4 and 4 are each 4 units from 0, even though they are on the opposite sides of 0. The absolute value of 4 is 4; it is written with vertical bar symbols, |4| = 4. The absolute value of -4 is 4; it is also written with vertical bar symbols, |-4| = 4.

Create Your Left-Hand Notebook Page

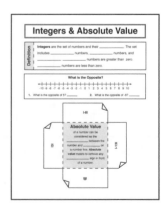

Step 1: Cut out the title and glue it to the top of the notebook page.

Step 2: Fill in the blanks on the *Definitions* flap piece. Cut out the piece. Apply glue to the back of the gray tab and attach it below the title. Under the flap, provide an example for the definition.

Step 3: Answer the questions on the *What is the Opposite?* piece. Apply glue to the back and attach it below the definition piece. Graph the numbers and their opposites on the number line.

Step 4: Fill in the blanks on the *Absolute Value* flap book. Cut out the book. Apply glue to the gray center section and attach it at the bottom of the page. Under each flap, write the absolute value.

Integers & Absolute Value

Definition

Integers are the set of numbers and their _____. The set includes _____ numbers, _____ numbers, and _____. _____ numbers are greater than zero. _____ numbers are less than zero.

What is the Opposite?

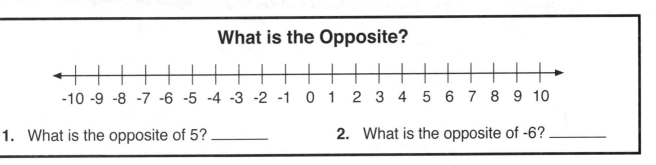

1. What is the opposite of 5? _____
2. What is the opposite of -6? _____

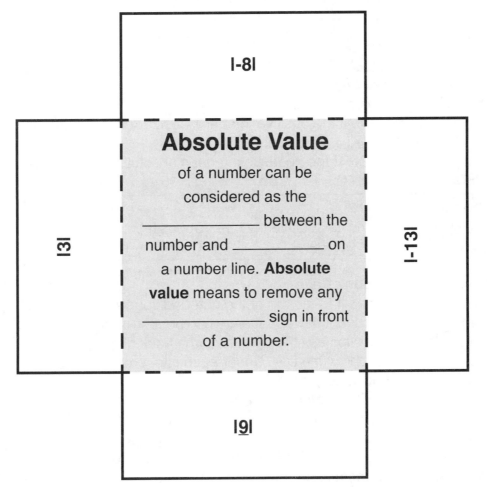

|-8|

|3|

Absolute Value

of a number can be considered as the _____ between the number and _____ on a number line. **Absolute value** means to remove any _____ sign in front of a number.

|-13|

|9|

Student Instructions: Adding & Subtracting Integers

Read the following information. Cut out the mini-lesson and attach it to the right-hand page of your interactive notebook. Use what you have learned to create the left-hand page.

Mini-Lesson

Adding & Subtracting Integers

Terms You Should Know
- **Additive inverse:** the opposite of a given number. For example, 3 is the opposite of -3. The sum of any number and its additive inverse is zero.
  - **Example:** $3 + (-3) = 0$.
- **Absolute value:** the distance between the number and zero on a number line. Since distance cannot be negative, the absolute value of every number will be either positive or zero.
  - **Example:** The absolute value of -2 is 2.

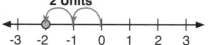

2 Units

-3   -2   -1   0   1   2   3

Working With Integers

Adding Integers/Same Sign
When adding integers with the same sign, you add their absolute values.
  • The sum will be positive if both integers are positive.
     Examples: $(+) + (+) = (+)$ **so** $5 + 3 = 8$
  • The sum will be negative if both integers are negative.
     Examples: $(-) + (-) = (-)$ **so** $-6 + (-4) = -10$

Adding Integers/Different Signs
When adding integers with different signs, you subtract their absolute values.
  • The sum will be positive if the positive integer's absolute value is greater.
     Examples: $(+) + (-) = (+)$ **so** $6 + (-1) = 5$
  • The sum will be negative if the negative integer's absolute value is greater.
     Examples: $(-) + (+) = (-)$ **so** $-6 + 1 = -5$

Subtracting Integers Subtract an integer by adding its additive inverse, (opposite).   **Examples:** $3 - 8 = 3 + (-8) = -5$ $-4 - (11) = -4 + (-11) = -15$

Create Your Left-Hand Notebook Page

Step 1: Cut out the title and glue it to the top of the notebook page.

Step 2: Fill in the blanks and cut out the *Vocabulary* flap book. Cut on the solid line to create two flaps. Apply glue to the back of the gray tab and attach it below the title. Under each flap, provide an example of the vocabulary word.

Step 3: Cut out the *Adding & Subtracting Integers Rules* flap book. Cut on the solid lines to create three flaps. Apply glue to the back of the gray tab and attach at the bottom of the page.

Step 4: Solve the problem pieces. Cut out the pieces. Apply glue to the backs and attach them under the correct rule flap.

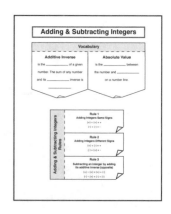

Adding & Subtracting Integers

Vocabulary

Additive Inverse

is the _____ of a given

number. The sum of any number

and its _____ inverse is

_____.

Absolute Value

is the _____ between

the number and _____

on a number line.

Adding & Subtracting Integers Rules

Rule 1
Adding Integers Same Signs

$(+) + (+) = +$

$(-) + (-) = -$

Rule 2
Adding Integers Different Signs

$(+) + (-) = +$

$(-) + (+) = -$

Rule 3
Subtracting an interger by adding its additive inverse (opposite)

$(+) - (+) = (+) + (-)$

$(-) - (+) = (-) + (-)$

1. $-34 + 52 =$

2. $-7 + -64 =$

3. $-23 - 10 =$

4. $15 - (-12) =$

5. $52 + (-81) =$

Student Instructions: Adding & Subtracting Using Mathematical Properties

Read the following information. Cut out the mini-lesson and attach it to the right-hand page of your interactive notebook. Use what you have learned to create the left-hand page.

Mini-Lesson

Adding & Subtracting Using Mathematical Properties

The mathematical properties of operations are rules of addition and subtraction that make solving problems easier.

Addition and Subtraction Properties		
Property	**Description**	**Examples**
Commutative Property of Addition	The order in which numbers are added does not change the sum.	$7 + 5 = 5 + 7$
Associative Property of Addition	The way in which numbers are grouped when added does not change the sum.	$(-4 + 6) + 2 = -4 + (6 + 2)$
Identity Property of Addition and Subtraction	The sum or difference of any number and 0 is that number.	$8 + 0 = 8$ $8 - 0 = 8$
Additive Inverse Property	The sum of any number and its additive inverse is 0.	$9 + (-9) = 0$
Addition and Subtraction Inverse Properties	Addition and subtraction operations cancel each other out.	$5 + 3 = 8$ so, $8 - 3 = 5$ $9 - 2 = 7$ so, $7 + 2 = 9$

Create Your Left-Hand Notebook Page

Step 1: Cut out the title and glue it to the top of the notebook page.

Step 2: Fill in the blanks on the *Mathematical Properties* flap book. Cut out the book. Cut on the solid lines to create five flaps. Apply glue to the back of the gray tab and attach it below the title.

Step 3: Cut out the five cards. Apply glue to the back of each card and attach them under the correct mathematical properties flap.

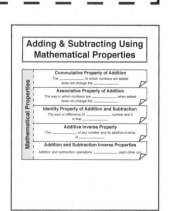

Adding & Subtracting Using Mathematical Properties

Mathematical Properties

Commutative Property of Addition

The _____ in which numbers are added
does not change the _____.

Associative Property of Addition

The way in which numbers are _____ when added
does not change the _____.

Identity Property of Addition and Subtraction

The sum or difference of _____ number and 0
is that _____.

Additive Inverse Property

The _____ of any number and its additive inverse
is _____.

Addition and Subtraction Inverse Properties

Addition and subtraction operations _____ each other out.

Card A $1,324 - 0 = 1,324$
                  $0 + 1,324 = 1,324$

Card B
                  $14 + (-14) = 0$

Card C
                  $75 + 5 = 5 + 75$

Card D $10 - 2 = 8$ so, $8 + 2 = 10$
                  $12 + 5 = 17$ so, $17 - 5 = 12$

Card E
                  $(-6 + 7) + 3 = -6 + (7 + 3)$

Student Instructions: Working With Rational Numbers

Read the following information. Cut out the mini-lesson and attach it to the right-hand page of your interactive notebook. Use what you have learned to create the left-hand page.

Mini-Lesson

Working With Rational Numbers

Rational numbers include fractions and decimals. Any fraction can be expressed as a decimal by dividing the numerator by the denominator. A **terminating decimal** is a decimal number that ends. It's a decimal with a limited number of digits. A **repeating decimal**, or recurring decimal, is a decimal number in which a pattern of one or more digits is repeated indefinitely.

Fraction to a Decimal	Repeating Decimals
Divide the numerator by the denominator. **Example:** $\frac{1}{4}$ written as a decimal $$4 \overline{\smash{)}1.00}$$ $$\begin{array}{r} 0.25 \\ \hline -8 \\ \hline 20 \\ -20 \\ \hline 0 \end{array}$$ denominator · · · numerator Therefore, $\frac{1}{4} = 0.25$	To express $\frac{2}{3}$ as a decimal, divide 2 by 3. The quotient is a repeating decimal. Draw a bar over the digit or digits that repeat. $$0.6666 = 0.\overline{6}$$ $$3 \overline{\smash{)}2.0000}$$ $$\begin{array}{r} -18 \\ \hline 20 \\ -18 \\ \hline 20 \\ -18 \\ \hline 20 \\ -18 \\ \hline 2 \end{array}$$
Decimal to a Fraction	**Terminating Decimals**
Read the decimal aloud. Write the fraction. Simplify. **Example:** 0.6 written as a fraction 0.6 is read as "six tenths" Therefore, $0.6 = \frac{6}{10} = \frac{3}{5}$	To express $\frac{1}{5}$ as a decimal, divide 1 by 5. Divide until the remainder is zero. $$5 \overline{\smash{)}1.0}$$ $$\begin{array}{r} 0.2 \\ \hline -10 \\ \hline 0 \end{array}$$

Create Your Left-Hand Notebook Page

Step 1: Cut out the title and glue it to the top of the notebook page.

Step 2: Cut out the *Rational Number Rule* flap book. Cut on the solid lines to create four flaps. Apply glue to the gray center section and attach it below the title.

Step 3: Under each flap, convert the fraction to a decimal and identify the decimal as terminating or repeating. Show your work.

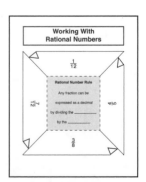

Working With Rational Numbers

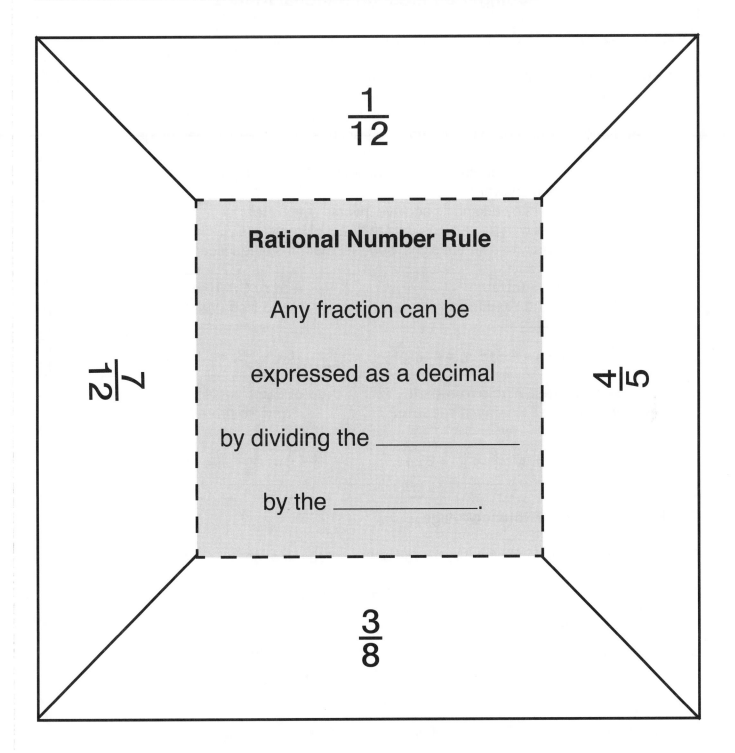

$\dfrac{1}{12}$

$\dfrac{7}{12}$

$\dfrac{4}{5}$

Rational Number Rule

Any fraction can be

expressed as a decimal

by dividing the _____

by the _____.

$\dfrac{3}{8}$

Student Instructions: Adding & Subtracting Rational Numbers

Read the following information. Cut out the mini-lesson and attach it to the right-hand page of your interactive notebook. Use what you have learned to create the left-hand page.

Mini-Lesson

Adding & Subtracting Rational Numbers

Rational numbers include integers, fractions, and decimals.

Tips for Adding and Subtracting Rational Numbers
- Convert rational numbers to the same form to add or subtract.
- Line up decimal points; move decimal point straight down in the answer.
- Add and subtract positive and negative fractions like whole number integers.
- Make sure fractions have a common denominator to add or subtract.
- Convert mixed numbers to improper fractions before adding and subtracting.
- Simplify fraction answers.
- Subtract integers by adding its additive inverse (opposite).
- Adding integers with same signs, add their absolute values.
- Adding integers with different signs, subtract their absolute values.

Add or Subtract Decimals and Fractions	Add or Subtract Decimals and Negative Numbers
$4.1 + \frac{2}{6} = 4\frac{1}{10} + \frac{2}{6} = 4\frac{3}{30} + \frac{10}{30} = 4\frac{13}{30}$	$6.8 - (-3) = 6.8 + 3.0 = 9.8$
Add or Subtract Whole Numbers and Negative and Positive Fractions	**Add or Subtract Negative Fractions and Positive Fractions**
$24 - (-\frac{9}{8}) = 24 + \frac{9}{8} = \frac{192}{8} + \frac{9}{8} = \frac{201}{8} = 25\frac{1}{8}$	$\frac{6}{-8} - \frac{4}{5} = -\frac{30}{40} - \frac{32}{40} = -\frac{62}{40} = -\frac{31}{20} = -1\frac{11}{20}$

Create Your Left-Hand Notebook Page

Step 1: Cut out the title and glue it to the top of the notebook page.

Step 2: Evaluate each expression on the *Which Tip?* flap book. Place the value on the front of the flap.

Step 3: Cut out the *Which Tip?* flap book. Cut on the solid lines to create six flaps. Apply glue to the back of the gray center section and attach it below the title.

Step 4: Under each flap, write the tip or tips that helped you solve the problem.

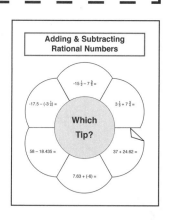

Adding & Subtracting Rational Numbers

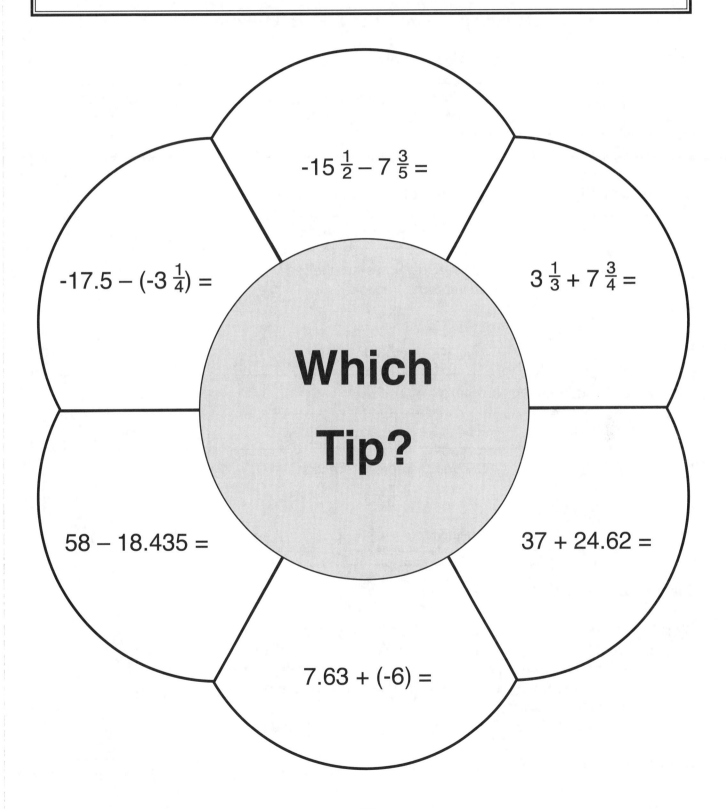

$-15\frac{1}{2} - 7\frac{3}{5} =$

$-17.5 - (-3\frac{1}{4}) =$

$3\frac{1}{3} + 7\frac{3}{4} =$

Which Tip?

$58 - 18.435 =$

$37 + 24.62 =$

$7.63 + (-6) =$

Student Instructions: Multiplying Fractions & Mixed Numbers

Read the following information. Cut out the mini-lesson and attach it to the right-hand page of your interactive notebook. Use what you have learned to create the left-hand page.

Mini-Lesson

Multiplying Fractions & Mixed Numbers

Steps to Multiply a Fraction by a Fraction

Problem	Multiply the Numerators, Multiply the Denominators	Simplify
$\frac{4}{5} \times \frac{5}{6}$	$\frac{4}{5} \times \frac{5}{6} = \frac{20}{30}$	$\frac{2}{3}$

Steps to Multiply a Fraction by a Whole Number

Problem	Rewrite and Multiply	Simplify
$12 \times \frac{7}{8}$	Rewrite the whole number as an improper fraction. $$\frac{12}{1} \times \frac{7}{8}$$ Multiply. $\frac{12}{1} \times \frac{7}{8} = \frac{84}{8}$	$10\frac{1}{2}$

Steps to Multiply Mixed Numbers

Problem	Rewrite and Multiply	Simplify
$3\frac{1}{2} \times 2\frac{1}{2}$	Convert to improper fraction. $$\frac{7}{2} \times \frac{5}{2}$$ Multiply. $\frac{7}{2} \times \frac{5}{2} = \frac{35}{4}$	$8\frac{3}{4}$

Create Your Left-Hand Notebook Page

Step 1: Cut out the title and glue it to the top of the notebook page.

Step 2: Cut out the *Multiply a Fraction by a Fraction, Multiply a Fraction by a Whole Number,* and *Multiply Mixed Numbers* flap books. Apply glue to the gray center section of each book and attach them below the title.

Step 3: Under each "Steps" flap, write the steps to solving the problem on the right.

Step 4: Under each problem flap, solve the problem. Show your work.

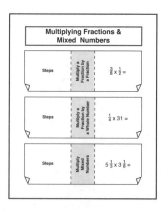

Multiplying Fractions & Mixed Numbers

Steps	Multiply a Fraction by a Fraction	$\dfrac{3}{8} \times \dfrac{1}{2} =$

Steps	Multiply a Fraction by a Whole Number	$\dfrac{1}{4} \times 31 =$

Steps	Multiply Mixed Numbers	$5\dfrac{1}{3} \times 3\dfrac{1}{8} =$

Student Instructions: Multiplying & Dividing Using Mathematical Properties

Read the following information. Cut out the mini-lesson and attach it to the right-hand page of your interactive notebook. Use what you have learned to create the left-hand page.

Mini-Lesson

Multiplying & Dividing Using Mathematical Properties

The properties of operations are rules of multiplication and division that make solving problems easier.

Properties of Operations	Definition	Example
Commutative Property of Multiplication	The order in which numbers are multiplied does not change the product.	$6 \times 2 = 2 \times 6$ $12 = 12$
Associative Property of Multiplication	The way in which numbers are grouped when multiplied does not change the product.	$(4 \times 3) \times 5 = 4 \times (3 \times 5)$ $12 \times 5 = 4 \times 15$ $60 = 60$
Identity Property of Multiplication and Division	Any number multiplied or divided by 1 is that number.	$14 \times 1 = 14$ $14 \div 1 = 14$
Inverse Property of Multiplication and Division	Multiplication and division are opposite operations that undo each other.	$4 \times 6 = 24$ $24 \div 6 = 4$ and $24 \div 4 = 6$ $56 \div 7 = 8$ $7 \times 8 = 56$ and $8 \times 7 = 56$
Zero Product Property	Any number multiplied by 0 is zero.	$7 \times 0 = 0$
Distributive Property	When you have both the operation of addition and the operation of multiplication to perform, you can decide which to do first.	$4 \times (5 + 2) = (4 \times 5) + (4 \times 2)$ $4 \times 7 = 20 + 8$ $28 = 28$

Create Your Left-Hand Notebook Page

Step 1: Cut out the title and glue it to the top of the notebook page.

Step 2: Cut out the *Multiplying & Dividing Using Mathematical Properties* flap book. Cut on the solid lines to create six flaps. Apply glue to the gray center section and attach it below the title.

Step 3: Under each flap, identify and explain the property used in each problem.

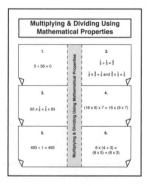

Multiplying & Dividing Using Mathematical Properties

1.

$0 \div 56 = 0$

2.

$\frac{1}{4} \div \frac{1}{3} = \frac{3}{4}$

$\frac{1}{3} \times \frac{3}{4} = \frac{1}{4}$ and $\frac{3}{4} \times \frac{1}{3} = \frac{1}{4}$

3.

$85 \times \frac{7}{6} = \frac{7}{6} \times 85$

4.

$(16 \times 9) \times 7 = 16 \times (9 \times 7)$

5.

$493 \div 1 = 493$

6.

$6 \times (4 + 3) =$
$(6 \times 5) + (6 \times 3)$

Multiplying & Dividing Using Mathematical Properties

Student Instructions: Multiplying & Dividing Integers

Read the following information. Cut out the mini-lesson and attach it to the right-hand page of your interactive notebook. Use what you have learned to create the left-hand page.

Mini-Lesson

Multiplying and Dividing Integers

When multiplying and dividing integers, it is important to pay attention to the signs and remember two rules.

Rule 1: Multiplying and Dividing If the Signs Are the Same, the Answer Is Always Positive	
Example: 8 x 8 = 64 (+) x (+) = +	**Example:** 48 ÷ 6 = 8 (+) ÷ (+) = (+)
Example: -7 x -7 = 49 (-) x (-) = +	**Example:** -12 ÷ -2 = 6 (-) ÷ (-) = (+)
Rule 2: Multiplying and Dividing If the Signs Are Different, the Answer Is Always Negative	
Example: 5 x -5 = -25 (+) x (-) = -	**Example:** 99 ÷ -9 = -11 (+) ÷ (-) = -
Example: -6 x 6 = -36 (-) x (+) = -	**Example:** -28 ÷ 7 = -4 (-) ÷ (+) = -

Create Your Left-Hand Notebook Page

Step 1: Cut out the title and glue it to the top of the notebook page.

Step 2: Fill in the blanks on the *Rule 1* and the *Rule 2* pocket holders. Cut out the two pocket holders. Fold back the gray tabs on the dotted lines. Apply glue to the gray side of the tab and attach each pocket holder below the title.

Step 3: Evaluate the eight expressions. Cut apart the expression strips. Place each strip in the correct pocket holder.

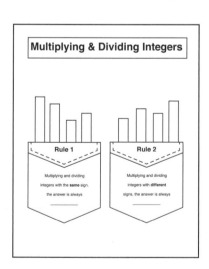

Multiplying & Dividing Integers

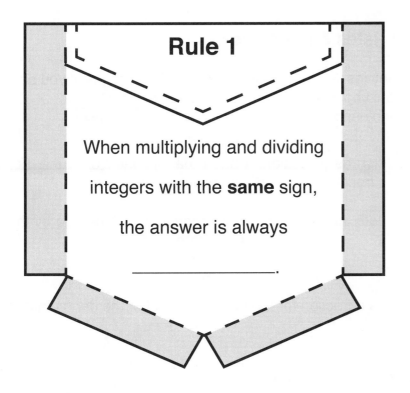

Rule 1

When multiplying and dividing

integers with the **same** sign,

the answer is always

_____.

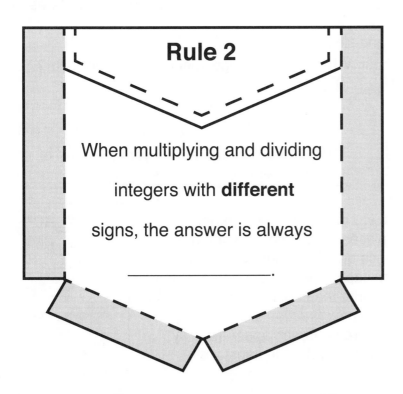

Rule 2

When multiplying and dividing

integers with **different**

signs, the answer is always

_____.

5.	-32 ÷ 4
6.	52 x 9
7.	-84 ÷ (-4)
8.	-267 x (-17)

1.	-13 x (-5)
2.	939 ÷ 3
3.	132 ÷ (-11)
4.	49 x (-27)

Student Instructions: Unit Rates & Fractions

Read the following information. Cut out the mini-lesson and attach it to the right-hand page of your interactive notebook. Use what you have learned to create the left-hand page.

Mini-Lesson

Unit Rates & Fractions

A **rate** is a ratio that compares two quantities that are in different units. For example, if you paid $1.39 for an 8-ounce drink, the rate could be written as $1.39:8 ounces or $\frac{\$1.39}{8\text{-ounces}}$. The first term is measured in dollars and cents; the second term in ounces.

A **unit rate** is a ratio for one unit. Written as a fraction, it has a denominator of 1 unit. For example, 35 miles per hour written as a fraction would be $\frac{35\text{ miles}}{1\text{ hour}}$.

To convert a rate to a unit rate, divide both the numerator and denominator of the rate by the denominator. **Example:**

Rate		Unit Rate
$\frac{16\text{ miles}}{4\text{ minutes}}$	$\begin{array}{c}(\div 4)\\(\div 4)\end{array} =$	$\frac{4\text{ miles}}{1\text{ minute}}$

A **complex fraction** is a fraction that has a fraction for the numerator and/or the denominator.
Examples: $\dfrac{20}{\frac{1}{4}}$ $\dfrac{\frac{1}{2}}{6}$ $\dfrac{1\frac{1}{4}}{\frac{1}{2}}$

Steps to Convert a Complex Fraction to a Unit Rate
1. Rewrite fraction horizontally as a division problem.
2. Rewrite the problem using the reciprocal. Note: If dividing by a whole number, first write as a fraction with a denominator of 1. If dividing with a mixed number, first write as an improper fraction.
3. Solve the problem by multiplying and simplifying.

Example: Sue ran $1\frac{1}{4}$ miles in $\frac{1}{4}$ hour. What is her average speed in miles per hour?

$$\frac{1\frac{1}{4}\text{ miles}}{\frac{1}{4}} = 1\frac{1}{4} \div \frac{1}{4}$$
$$= \frac{5}{4} \div \frac{1}{4}$$
$$= \frac{5}{4} \times \frac{4}{1}$$
$$= \frac{20}{4} \text{ or } 5 \qquad \text{Therefore, Sue ran at an average speed of 5 miles per hour.}$$

Create Your Left-Hand Notebook Page

Step 1: Cut out the title and glue it to the top of the notebook page.

Step 2: Cut out the three *Question* flap pieces. Attach each by the gray tab under the title and answer each question under each flap.

Step 3: Fill in the blanks on the *Definition* flap piece. Cut out and attach it below the *Question* flap pieces. Under the flap, provide an example.

Step 4: Cut out the *Steps to Convert a Complex Fraction to a Unit Rate* flap book. Cut on the solid lines to create three flaps. Attach by the gray tab at the bottom of the page. Under the flaps, write each step to converting the problem on the gray tab.

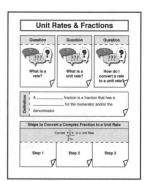

Unit Rates & Fractions

Question	Question	Question
 **What is a rate?**	 **What is a unit rate?**	 **How do I convert a rate to a unit rate?**

Definition

A _____ fraction is a fraction that has a

_____ for the numerator and/or the

denominator.

Steps to Convert a Complex Fraction to a Unit Rate		
Convert $\dfrac{8\frac{1}{2}\text{ ft.}}{\frac{3}{4}\text{ hr.}}$ to a Unit Rate		
Step 1	**Step 2**	**Step 3**

Student Instructions: Proportional Relationships

Read the following information. Cut out the mini-lesson and attach it to the right-hand page of your interactive notebook. Use what you have learned to create the left-hand page.

Mini-Lesson

Proportional Relationships

A **ratio** is a comparison of two quantities (numbers or measurements) to each other. A **proportion** is two equal ratios. There are several ways to determine if two ratios have a proportional relationship.

Compare Simplest Form of Each Ratio: Write the ratios as fractions and then simplify.

   Example: Compare the ratios 1:5 and 5:25.

$$\frac{1}{5} \text{ and } \frac{5}{25}$$

$$\frac{1}{5} \text{ and } \frac{5 \div 5}{25 \div 5} = \frac{1}{5}$$

$\frac{1}{5}$ is in simplest form. $\frac{5}{25}$ can be simplified by dividing the numerator and denominator by the greatest common factor, 5. Both fractions simplify to $\frac{1}{5}$. Therefore, the ratios 1:5 and 5:25 are equal and in a proportional relationship.

Cross Product: First write the ratios as fractions and then cross multiply.

   Example: Compare 2:5 and 4:10

$$\frac{2}{5} \diagdown \frac{4}{10} = \frac{20}{20}$$

The cross products, 2 x 10 = 20 and 4 x 5 = 20, are equal. So, the ratios are equal and in a proportional relationship.

Graphing: Another way to determine whether two quantities are proportional is to plot the quantities on a graph. The two quantities are proportional if the graph is a straight line through the origin.

time (min.)	distance (in.)
x	y
0	0
1	5
2	10
3	15
4	20

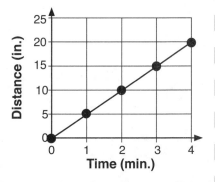

Create Your Left-Hand Notebook Page

Step 1: Cut out the title and glue it to the top of the notebook page.

Step 2: Cut out the *What's the Difference?* flap book. Apply glue to the back of the gray center section and attach it below the title. Under each flap, write the definition.

Step 3: Cut out the *Is the Relationship Proportional?* flap book. Apply glue to the back of the gray tab and attach it below the first flap book. Under each flap, explain your answer.

Step 4: Plot the quantities from the table on the graph. Cut out the table and graph. Apply glue to the back of both and attach them at the bottom of the page.

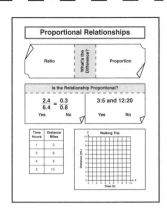

Proportional Relationships

Ratio	What's the Difference?	Proportion

Is the Relationship Proportional?

$$\frac{2.4}{6.4} = \frac{0.3}{0.8}$$

Yes   No

3:5 and 12:20

Yes   No

Time Hours	Distance Miles
1	2
3	6
4	8
5	10

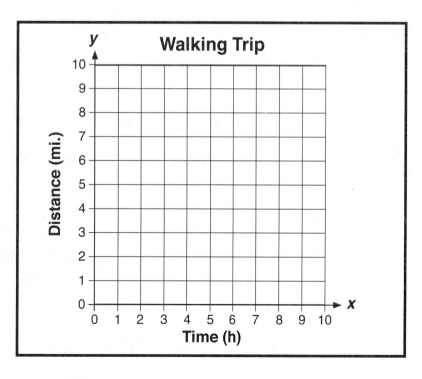

Student Instructions: Constant of Proportionality

Read the following information. Cut out the mini-lesson and attach it to the right-hand page of your interactive notebook. Use what you have learned to create the left-hand page.

Mini-Lesson

Constant of Proportionality

The **constant of proportionality** is also known as the **unit rate**. The **constant** or rate of change is the value (number) that is fixed or does not change in a proportional relationship. The equation for finding the constant of proportionality can be written two ways.

Example: $y = kx$ or $k = \dfrac{y}{x}$

The constant (k) tells you how much the value of y increases as the value of x increases.

> **Constant of Proportionality Equation**
>
> $y = kx$ $y = 4x$
>
> constant of proportionality

Finding the Constant of Proportionality

    Examples: What is the constant of proportionality for the value in the table and graph?

Table

x	1	5	3
y	3	15	9

Since $y = kx$, we can say $k = \dfrac{y}{x}$

Therefore:

$k = \dfrac{3}{1}$ or $k = 3$

$k = \dfrac{15}{5}$ or $k = 3$

$k = \dfrac{9}{3}$ or $k = 3$

So, the constant (k) is 3.

Graph

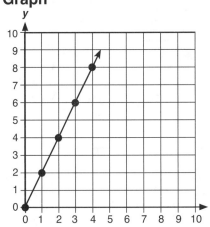

Since $y = kx$, we can say $k = \dfrac{y}{x}$

Therefore:

$k = \dfrac{2}{1}$ or $k = 2$

$k = \dfrac{4}{2}$ or $k = 2$

$k = \dfrac{6}{3}$ or $k = 2$

$k = \dfrac{8}{4}$ or $k = 2$

So, the constant (k) is 2.

Create Your Left-Hand Notebook Page

Step 1: Cut out the title and glue it to the top of the notebook page.

Step 2: Fill in the blanks on the *Constant of Proportionality* flap book. Cut out the book. Cut on the solid line to create two bottom flaps. Apply glue to the back of the gray center section and attach it below the title.

Step 3: Under the *Definition* flap, explain what the constant in an equation tells you. Under each of the equation flaps, write one way the constant of proportionality equation can be written.

Step 4: Cut out the *What is the Constant?* flap book. Apply glue to the back of the gray center section and attach it at the bottom of the page. Under each flap, identify the constant for the values given.

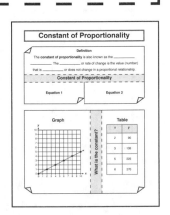

Constant of Proportionality

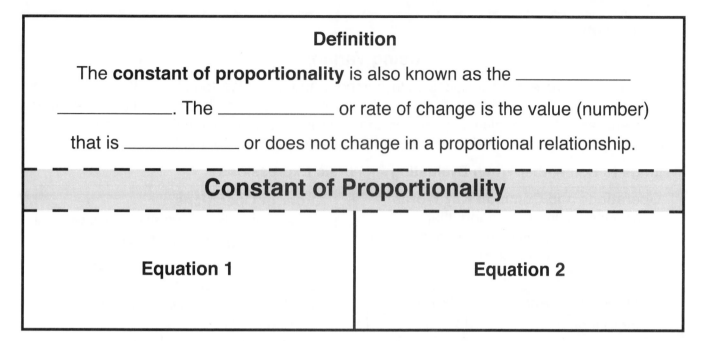

Definition

The **constant of proportionality** is also known as the _____

_____. The _____ or rate of change is the value (number)

that is _____ or does not change in a proportional relationship.

Constant of Proportionality

| Equation 1 | Equation 2 |

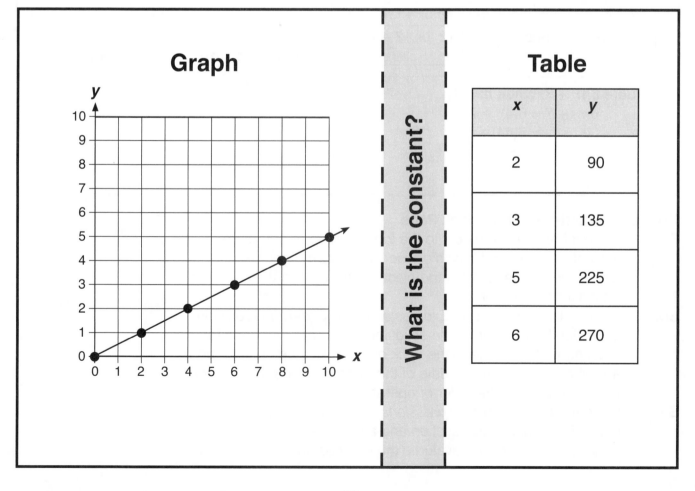

Graph

What is the constant?

Table

x	y
2	90
3	135
5	225
6	270

Student Instructions: Using Variables

Read the following information. Cut out the mini-lesson and attach it to the right-hand page of your interactive notebook. Use what you have learned to create the left-hand page.

Mini-Lesson

Using Variables

An **algebraic expression** includes both numbers and variables together with at least one arithmetic operation. For example, $2x - 3$. A **variable** is a symbol (letter of the alphabet) that represents an unknown value in an expression. Expressions may have more than one variable. For example: $3x + y$. A **coefficient** is a number used to multiply a variable.

Things to Remember When Evaluating Algebraic Expressions

Operations and Common Key Words
Addition: sum, increase, more than
Subtraction: difference, less than, decrease
Multiplication: product, times, double
Division: quotient, divide

Mathematical Phrase	Expression
2 more than 3	$2 + 3$
6 less than x	$x - 6$
product of 4 and a number	$4n$ or $4 \cdot n$
quotient of 12 and x	$\dfrac{12}{x}$ or $12 \div x$

Order of Operations
Follow the order of operation laws when evaluating algebraic expressions.

1. Evaluate inside grouping symbols.
2. Evaluate powers.
3. Multiply and divide in order from left to right.
4. Add and subtract in order from left to right.

Evaluate $6m^3 + 7$, when $m = 4$
$$6m^3 + 7 = 6(4)^3 + 7$$
$$= 6(64) + 7$$
$$= 384 + 7$$
$$= 391$$

Evaluate $\dfrac{12}{x} + 9y$, when $x = 3$ and $y = 8$
$$\frac{12}{x} + 9y = \frac{12}{3} + 9(8)$$
$$= 4 + 72$$
$$= 76$$

Create Your Left-Hand Notebook Page

Step 1: Cut out the title and glue it to the top of the notebook page.

Step 2: Fill in the blanks and boxes on the *Parts of an Algebraic Expression* piece. Cut out the piece. Apply glue to the back and attach it below the title.

Step 3: Cut out the *Phrases and Expressions* and *Order of Operation Laws* flap books. Cut on the solid lines to create four flaps for each book. Apply glue to the back of the gray tabs on each book and attach them in the middle of the page. Under each flap, write the expression or the order of operation.

Step 4: Cut out the *Evaluating Expressions* flap book. Apply glue to the back of the gray center section and attach it at the bottom of the page. Under each flap, evaluate the expression.

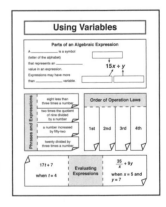

Using Variables

Parts of an Algebraic Expression

A _____ is a symbol (letter of the alphabet) that represents an _____ value in an expression. Expressions may have more than _____ variable.

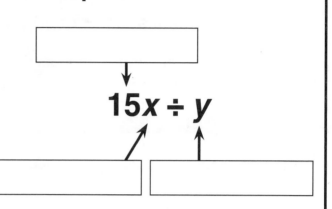

$$15x \div y$$

Phrases and Expressions

- eight less than three times a number
- two times the quotient of nine divided by a number
- a number increased by fifty-two
- twenty divided by three times a number

Order of Operation Laws

1st	2nd	3rd	4th

Evaluating Expressions

$17t + 7$ when $t = 4$

$\dfrac{35}{x} + 9y$ when $x = 5$ and $y = 7$

Student Instructions: Mathematical Properties & Equivalent Expressions

Read the following information. Cut out the mini-lesson and attach it to the right-hand page of your interactive notebook. Use what you have learned to create the left-hand page.

Mini-Lesson

Mathematical Properties & Equivalent Expressions

Understanding the **properties of operations** will help you identify, write, and evaluate equivalent expressions.

Properties of Operations	Definition	Symbols/Example	
Commutative Property of **Addition** or **Multiplication**	The order in which numbers are added or multiplied does not change the sum or product.	(+)	$a + b = b + a$ $5 + 3 = 3 + 5$
		(x)	$a \cdot b = b \cdot a$ $6 \cdot 2 = 2 \cdot 6$
Associative Property of **Addition** or **Multiplication**	The way in which numbers are grouped when they are added or multiplied does not change the sum or product.	(+)	$a + (b + c) = (a + b) + c$ $7 + (3 + 8) = (7 + 3) + 8$
		(x)	$a \cdot (b \cdot c) = (a \cdot b) \cdot c$ $4 \cdot (3 \cdot 5) = (4 \cdot 3) \cdot 5$
Distributive Property	When you multiply a **sum** or **difference** by a number, multiply each term inside the parentheses by the number outside the parentheses.	(+)	$a(b + c) = ab + ac$ $7(5 + 2) = 7 \cdot 5 + 7 \cdot 2$
		(−)	$a(b - c) = ab - ac$ $8(3 - 2) = 8 \cdot 3 - 8 \cdot 2$
Identity Property of Addition	The sum of any number and 0 is that number.		$a + 0 = a$ or $0 + a = a$ $3 + 0 = 3$ or $0 + 3 = 3$
Identity Property of Multiplication	Any number multiplied or divided by 1 is that number.	(x)	$a \cdot 1 = a$ or $1 \cdot a = a$ $14 \cdot 1 = 14$ or $1 \cdot 14 = 14$
		(÷)	$a \div 1 = 1$ $25 \div 1 = 25$
Zero Product Property	Any number multiplied by 0 is zero.		$a \cdot 0 = 0$ or $0 \cdot a = 0$ $7 \cdot 0 = 0$ or $0 \cdot 7 = 0$

Create Your Left-Hand Notebook Page

Step 1: Cut out the title and glue it to the top of the notebook page.

Step 2: Cut out the *Mathematical Properties and Equivalent Expressions* flap book. Apply glue to the back of the gray center section and attach it below the title.

Step 3: On each flap, write the equivalent expression. Under each flap, write the property used on the flap.

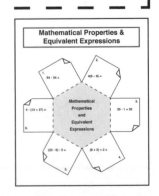

Mathematical Properties & Equivalent Expressions

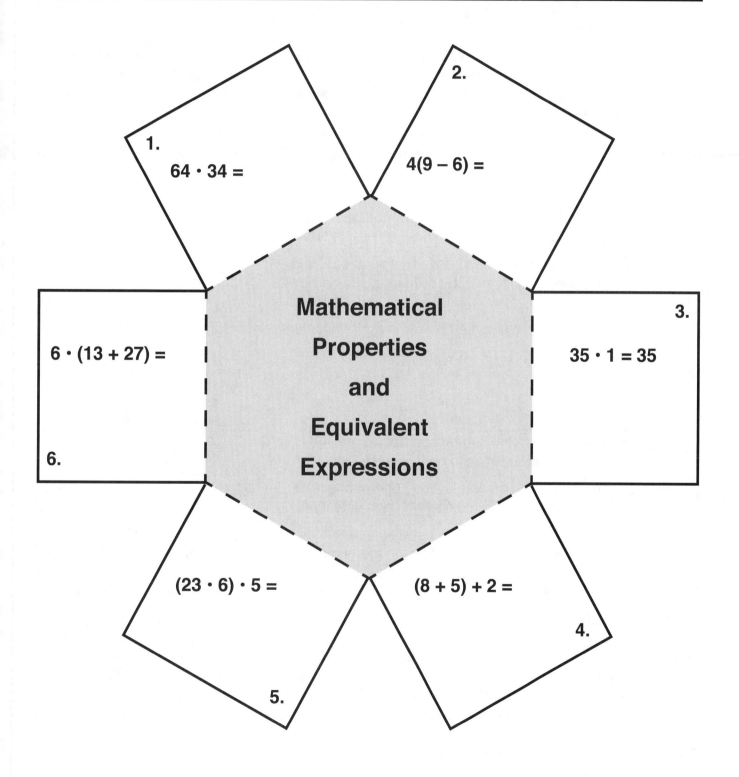

1.
$64 \cdot 34 =$

2.
$4(9 - 6) =$

Mathematical
Properties
and
Equivalent
Expressions

3.
$35 \cdot 1 = 35$

6.
$6 \cdot (13 + 27) =$

$(23 \cdot 6) \cdot 5 =$

5.

$(8 + 5) + 2 =$

4.

Student Instructions: Solving Two-Step Equations

Read the following information. Cut out the mini-lesson and attach it to the right-hand page of your interactive notebook. Use what you have learned to create the left-hand page.

Mini-Lesson

Solving Two-Step Equations

A **two-step equation** has two different operations to solve. When solving a two-step equation, you are using **inverse operations** to isolate the variable by doing the order of operations in reverse. It is very important to remember that what you do to one side of the "=", you must do to the other side.

Example 1

Solve $2a + 6 = 12$

Step 1: Undo addition and subtraction operations first.
Undo addition by subtracting 6 from each side.

Step 2: Undo multiplication and division operations next.
Undo the multiplication by dividing each side by 2.

$$\begin{array}{rcl} 2a + 6 &=& 12 \\ -6 &=& -6 \\ \hline 2a &=& 6 \end{array}$$

$$\begin{array}{rcl} \dfrac{2a}{2} &=& \dfrac{6}{2} \\ \text{Answer is} \quad a &=& 3 \end{array}$$

To check your answer, place the answer in the original equation. So, $2 \cdot 3 + 6 = 12$

Example 2

Solve $\dfrac{y}{4} - 3 = 2$

Step 1: Undo addition and subtraction operations first.
Undo subtraction by adding 3 to each side.

Step 2: Undo multiplication and division operations next.
Undo the division by multiplying each side by 4.

$$\begin{array}{rcl} \dfrac{y}{4} - 3 &=& 2 \\ +3 &=& +3 \\ \hline \dfrac{y}{4} &=& 5 \end{array}$$

$$\begin{array}{rcl} 4 \cdot \dfrac{y}{4} &=& 5 \cdot 4 \\ \text{Answer is} \quad y &=& 20 \end{array}$$

To check your answer, place the answer in the original equation. So, $(20 \div 4) - 3 = 2$

Create Your Left-Hand Notebook Page

Step 1: Cut out the title and glue it to the top of the notebook page.

Step 2: Fill in the blanks on the *Two-Step Equations* flap book. Cut out the book. Cut on the solid lines to create four flaps. Apply glue to the back of the gray center section and attach it below the title.

Step 3: On the front of each flap, solve the equation, showing all the steps. Under each flap, show how to check your answer.

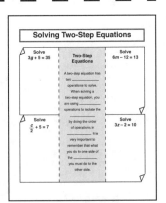

Solving Two-Step Equations

Solve

$3g + 5 = 35$

Solve

$\dfrac{c}{2} + 5 = 7$

Two-Step Equations

A two-step equation has two _____ operations to solve. When solving a two-step equation, you are using _____ operations to isolate the _____ by doing the order of operations in _____. It is very important to remember that what you do to one side of the _____, you must do to the other side.

Solve

$6m - 12 = 13$

Solve

$3z - 2 = 10$

Student Instructions: Two-Step Inequalities

Read the following information. Cut out the mini-lesson and attach it to the right-hand page of your interactive notebook. Use what you have learned to create the left-hand page.

Mini-Lesson

Two-Step Inequalities

Inequalities compare two quantities. A two-step inequality has two operations.

Example: $4x - 2 < 8$

multiplication   subtraction

Inequality Symbol	Number Line Symbol	Meaning
>	o—→	greater than, more than
<	←—o	less than, fewer than
≥	●—→	greater than or equal to
≤	←—●	less than or equal to

Inverse operations are opposite operations that undo each other, and they are used to solve two-step inequalities. Addition and subtraction are inverse operations. Multiplication and division are inverse operations.

Steps for Solving Two-Step Inequalities
Step 1: Undo the addition or subtraction operation.
Step 2: Undo the multiplication or division operation.
Step 3: Flip inequality symbol if you multiply or divide by a negative number.

> **Multiplying and Dividing Integers:**
> When the signs are different, the answer is **negative**. When the signs are the same, the answer is **positive**.

Solving and Graphing Two-Step Inequalities

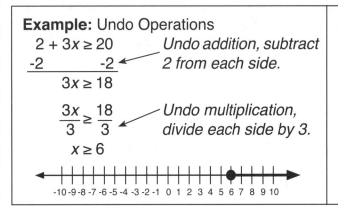

Example: Undo Operations

$2 + 3x \geq 20$
$\underline{-2 \qquad\qquad -2}$ ← *Undo addition, subtract 2 from each side.*
$3x \geq 18$

$\dfrac{3x}{3} \geq \dfrac{18}{3}$ ← *Undo multiplication, divide each side by 3.*

$x \geq 6$

-10-9-8-7-6-5-4-3-2-1 0 1 2 3 4 5 6 7 8 9 10

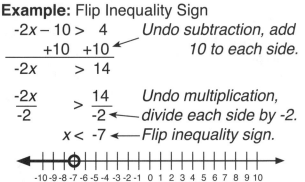

Example: Flip Inequality Sign

$-2x - 10 > 4$
$\underline{\qquad +10 \quad +10}$ ← *Undo subtraction, add 10 to each side.*
$-2x \qquad > 14$

$\dfrac{-2x}{-2} > \dfrac{14}{-2}$ ← *Undo multiplication, divide each side by -2.*

$x < -7$ ← *Flip inequality sign.*

-10-9-8-7-6-5-4-3-2-1 0 1 2 3 4 5 6 7 8 9 10

Create Your Left-Hand Notebook Page
Step 1: Cut out the title and glue it to the top of the notebook page.
Step 2: Cut out the *Inequality Symbols* flap book. Cut on the solid lines to create eight flaps. Apply glue to the gray tab and attach it below the title. Under each flap, write the meaning.
Step 3: Cut out the *Solving and Graphing Inequalities* flap book. Cut on the solid lines to create two flaps. Apply glue to the back of the gray tab and attach it at the bottom of the page. Under each flap, solve the inequality. On the front, graph the inequality.

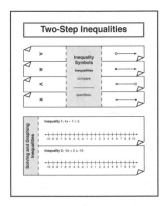

Two-Step Inequalities

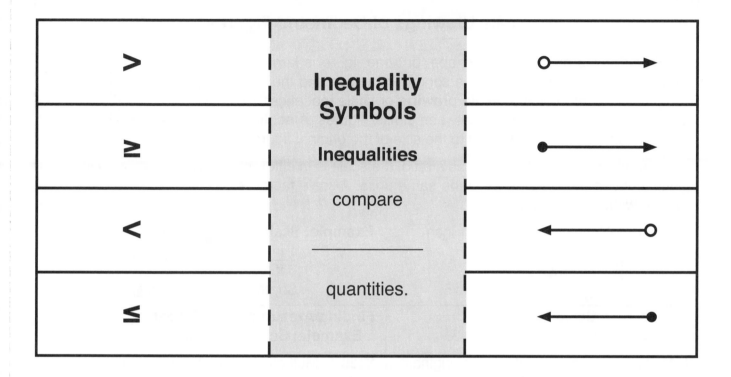

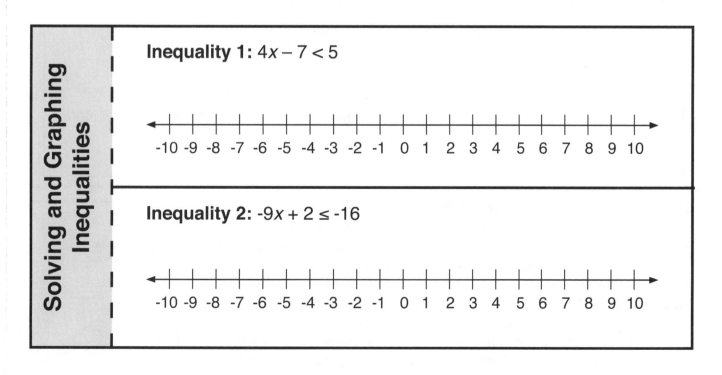

Student Instructions: Scale Drawings of Geometric Figures

Read the following information. Cut out the mini-lesson and attach it to the right-hand page of your interactive notebook. Use what you have learned to create the left-hand page.

Mini-Lesson

Scale Drawings of Geometric Figures

Similar figures are the same shape, but one figure is larger or smaller than the other. They have congruent angles and the side lengths are proportional. A **scale drawing** or scale model can be used to show the relationship between similar figures. A **scale** is a ratio of the size of the drawing to the size of the original figure.

A **scale factor** is a scale written as a ratio. If a scale is in different units, convert measurements to the same units. A scale factor is written without measurements.

Triangle: 4 in., 5 in., 3 in.   Triangle: 12 ft., 15 ft., 9 ft.

Scale 1:3
1 inch = distance of 3 feet

Example: Scale is 5 inches = 1 inch
$$\frac{5 \text{ inches}}{1 \text{ inch}} = 5$$
So, the scale factor is 5.

Example: Scale is 1 inch = 3 feet.
$$\frac{1 \text{ in.}}{3 \text{ ft.}} = \frac{1 \text{ in.}}{36 \text{ in.}}$$ Convert feet to inches.
So, the scale factor is $\frac{1}{36}$.

Drawing a Scale Model	**Finding Area of a Scale Model**
Example: The scale factor is 3.	**Example:** Scale Factor is 2.5

Drawing a Scale Model

Multiply each side length of the original figure by the scale factor.

Original   *Model*

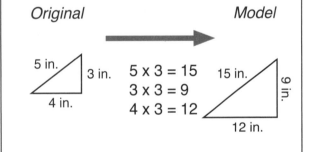

5 × 3 = 15
3 × 3 = 9
4 × 3 = 12

Finding Area of a Scale Model

Step 1: Multiply the length and width of the original figure by the scale factor.

Original   *Model*

4 cm, 2 cm → 10 cm, 5 cm

$L = 4 \times 2.5$
$W = 2 \times 2.5$

Step 2: Multiply the length and width of model.
10 × 5 = 50
So, $A = 50 \text{ cm}^2$

Create Your Left-Hand Notebook Page

Step 1: Cut out the title and glue it to the top of the notebook page.

Step 2: Fill in the blanks on the *Definitions* flap book. Cut on the solid line to create two flaps. Apply glue to the top gray section and attach it below the title. Under each flap, write the scale factor.

Step 3: Cut out the *Scale Factor* flap book. Cut on the solid lines to create four flaps. Apply glue to the back of the gray center section and attach it at the bottom of the page. Under flaps 1–4, use the scale factor to create a scale drawing for each figure. Label the new lengths. Under flaps 3 and 4, calculate the area of the new figure.

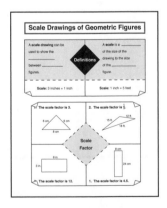

Scale Drawings of Geometric Figures

A **scale drawing** can be used to show the _____ between _____ figures.

Definitions

A **scale** is a _____ of the size of the drawing to the size of the _____ figure.

Scale: 3 inches = 1 inch

Scale: 1 inch = 5 feet

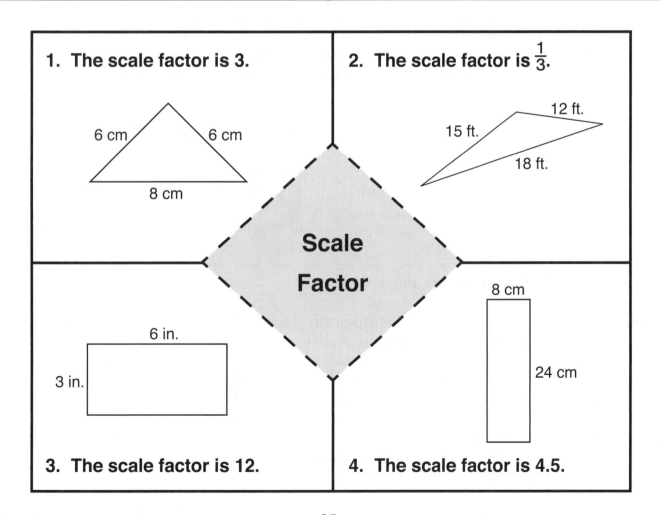

1. The scale factor is 3.

6 cm   6 cm
8 cm

2. The scale factor is $\frac{1}{3}$.

12 ft.
15 ft.
18 ft.

Scale Factor

3. The scale factor is 12.

6 in.
3 in.

4. The scale factor is 4.5.

8 cm
24 cm

Student Instructions: Three-Dimensional Figures

Read the following information. Cut out the mini-lesson and attach it to the right-hand page of your interactive notebook. Use what you have learned to create the left-hand page.

Mini-Lesson

Three-Dimensional Figures

A **three-dimensional (3-D)** figure has width, depth, and height.

Examples:

Classifying Three-Dimensional Figures

Polyhedrons	Non-Polyhedrons
Polyhedrons are classified based on information about their faces, edges, vertices, and the shape of the base. 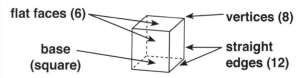	Non-polyhedrons are classified based on information about their bases and surfaces. 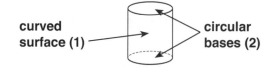

Cross Sections of Three-Dimensional Figures

A **plane** is a flat surface with no thickness. A **cross section** is the shape made when a plane cuts through a three-dimensional figure. There are two types of cross sections: horizontal and perpendicular (vertical).

Horizontal Cross Section

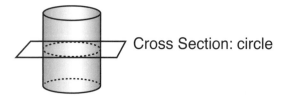 Cross Section: circle

Perpendicular Cross Section

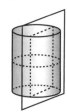 Cross Section: rectangle

Create Your Left-Hand Notebook Page

Step 1: Cut out the title and glue it to the top of the notebook page.

Step 2: Fill in the blanks on the *3-D* piece. Cut out the piece. Apply glue to the back and attach it below the title.

Step 3: Cut out the *What's the Difference?* flap book. Cut on the solid line to create two flaps. Apply glue to the back of the gray flap and attach it below the title. Under each flap, explain the difference.

Step 4: Complete the chart and cut it out. Apply glue to the back and attach it at the bottom of the page.

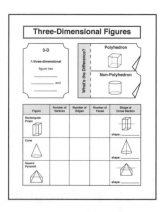

Three-Dimensional Figures

3-D

A **three-dimensional** figure has

_____,

_____, and

_____.

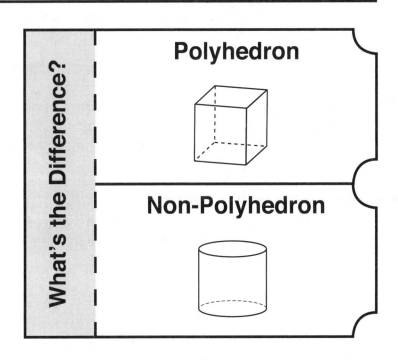

What's the Difference?

Polyhedron

Non-Polyhedron

Figure	Number of Vertices	Number of Edges	Number of Faces	Shape of Cross Section
Rectangular Prism				shape: _____
Cone				shape: _____
Square Pyramid				shape: _____

Student Instructions: Circumference

Read the following information. Cut out the mini-lesson and attach it to the right-hand page of your interactive notebook. Use what you have learned to create the left-hand page.

Mini-Lesson

Circumference

A **circle** is a round, two-dimensional figure. All points on the edge of the circle are the same distance from the **center point**. A circle is named by its center. For example, if point *B* is the center of the circle, then the name of the circle is circle *B*.

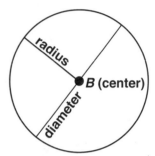

Circumference (C) is the distance around a circle. **Radius (r)** is a line segment that joins the center of the circle with any point on its circumference. **Diameter (d)** is a straight line passing through the center of a circle, ending at the circumference.

Finding Circumference

The circumference of a circle can be calculated using the diameter or radius of the circle. The formulas we can use appear below. In the formulas, the Greek letter π is called **pi**. The value of pi is rounded to 3.14.

$$C = πd \text{ (pi x diameter)} \quad \text{or} \quad C = 2πr \text{ (2 x pi x radius)}$$

Example: Diameter is 2 m	**Example:** Radius is 4 cm
$C = πd$ $C = 3.14 \times 2$ m $C = 6.28$ m	Step #1: Find Diameter $d = 2r$ $d = 2 \times 4$ cm $d = 8$ cm Step #2: Find Circumference $C = πd$ $C = 3.14 \times 8$ cm $C = 25.12$ cm

Create Your Left-Hand Notebook Page

Step 1: Cut out the title and glue it to the top of the notebook page.

Step 2: Fill in the blanks on the *Circle* flap book. Cut out the flap book. Cut on the solid lines to create four flaps. Apply glue to the back of the gray center section and attach it below the title. Under each flap, write the definition.

Step 3: Cut out the *Circumference* flap book. Cut on the solid lines to create four flaps. Apply glue to the back of the gray center section and attach it at the bottom of the page. Under each flap, write the formula and calculate the circumference.

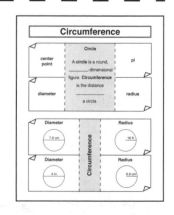

Circumference

center point	**Circle** A **circle** is a round, _____-dimensional figure. **Circumference** is the distance _____ a circle.	**pi**
diameter		**radius**

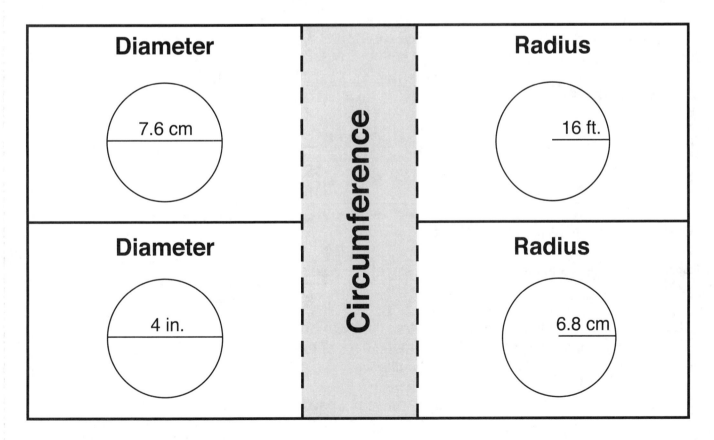

Diameter 7.6 cm	**Circumference**	**Radius** 16 ft.
Diameter 4 in.		**Radius** 6.8 cm

Student Instructions: Area of a Circle

Read the following information. Cut out the mini-lesson and attach it to the right-hand page of your interactive notebook. Use what you have learned to create the left-hand page.

Mini-Lesson

Area of a Circle

The **area** of a circle is the number of square units inside that circle. Area is measured in **square units** (sq. units) such as in.^{2}, ft.^{2}, cm^2, and m^2. The area of a circle is calculated by using the formulas below. The Greek letter π is called **pi**. The value of pi is approximately 3.14. To square a number means to multiply it by itself.

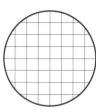

Finding Area of a Circle

When you know radius:	**When you know diameter:**
Area equals π (pi) times the radius squared:	**Step 1:** Calculate the radius — radius equals diameter divided by 2: $\dfrac{d}{2}$
Formula: $A = \pi r^2$ or $A = \pi \times r \times r$	
Example: Radius is 3 m	**Step 2:** Calculate area — Area equals π (pi) times the radius squared:
	Formula: $A = \pi r^2$ or $A = \pi \times r \times r$
	Example: Diameter is 8 m
$A = \pi \times r^2$	
$A = \pi \times r \times r$	
$A = 3.14 \times 3 \text{ m} \times 3 \text{ m}$	

$A = \pi \times r^2$
$A = \pi \times r \times r$
$A = 3.14 \times 3 \text{ m} \times 3 \text{ m}$
$A = 3.14 \times 9$
$A = 28.26 \text{ m}^2$

Step #1: Find Radius
$r = \dfrac{d}{2}$
$r = 8 \div 2$
$r = 4 \text{ m}$

Step #2: Find Area
$A = \pi \times r^2$
$A = \pi \times r \times r$
$A = 3.14 \times 4 \text{ m} \times 4 \text{ m}$
$A = 3.14 \times 16$
$A = 50.24 \text{ m}^2$

Create Your Left-Hand Notebook Page

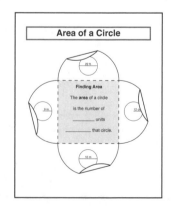

Step 1: Cut out the title and glue it to the top of the notebook page.

Step 2: Fill in the blanks on the *Finding Area* flap book. Then cut out the flap book and apply glue to the back of the gray center section. Attach it below the title.

Step 3: Under each flap, find the area. Show your work.

Area of a Circle

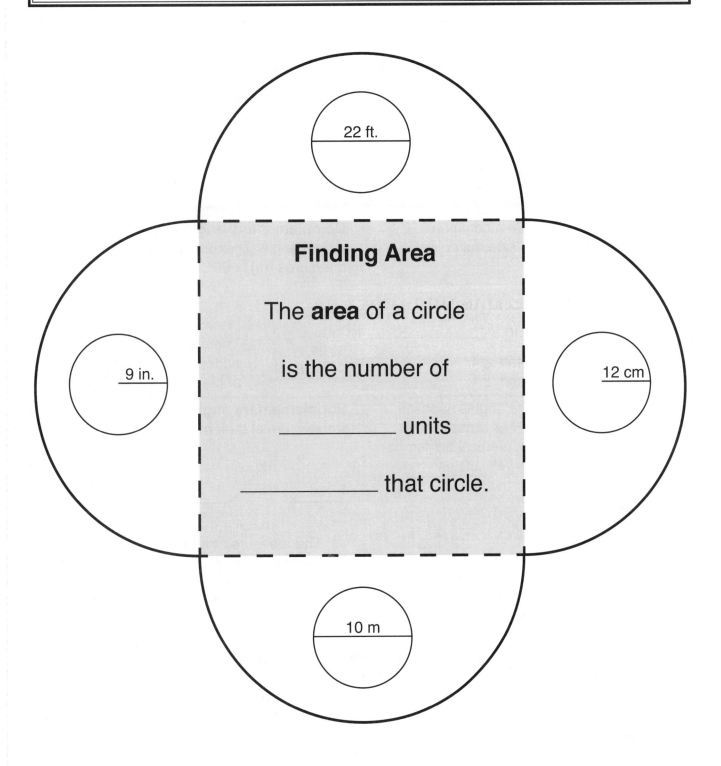

Finding Area

The **area** of a circle

is the number of

_____ units

_____ that circle.

22 ft.

9 in.

12 cm

10 m

Student Instructions: Angle Relationships

Read the following information. Cut out the mini-lesson and attach it to the right-hand page of your interactive notebook. Use what you have learned to create the left-hand page.

Mini-Lesson

Angle Relationships

Angles have two characteristics. First, all angles have two **sides** made from line segments, rays, or lines. Second, the sides share a common endpoint, called the **vertex**. The symbol used to represent an angle is ∠. There are several ways to name an angle. Use a number, ∠1. Write the vertex only, ∠A. Use the vertex as the middle letter and a point from each side, ∠BAC. Angles are often marked using an arc (⌒) or segment of a circle.

Types of Angles	

Adjacent angles share a common vertex and a common side but do not overlap.
 	
  Adjacent Angle Pairs
 ∠1 and ∠2
 ∠2 and ∠3
 ∠3 and ∠4
 ∠4 and ∠1
	Complementary angles together form a right angle. The sum of their measures (m) is 90°.
	
	  $m\angle A + m\angle B = 90°$
	
	 The measure of angle *A* added to the measure of angle *B* equals 90 degrees.

Vertical angles are the angles opposite each other when two lines cross. They share the same vertex. Vertical angles are congruent or equal (≅); angles **Vertical Angles** ∠1 and ∠3 ∠2 and ∠4 ∠1 ≅ ∠3 ∠2 ≅ ∠4	**Supplementary angles** are two angles whose sum of their measures (m) is 180°.  $m\angle A + m\angle B = 180°$ The measure of angle *A* added to the measure of angle *B* equals 180 degrees.

Create Your Left-Hand Notebook Page

Step 1: Cut out the title and glue it to the top of the notebook page.

Step 2: Cut out the *Angle Pairs* flap book. Cut on the solid lines to create four flaps. Apply glue to the back of the gray tab and attach it below the title. Under each flap, identify each angle pair as adjacent or vertical.

Step 3: Cut out the *Complementary or Supplementary?* flap book. Cut on the solid lines to create four flaps. Apply glue to the back of the gray tab and attach it at the bottom of the page. Under each flap, write the type of angle.

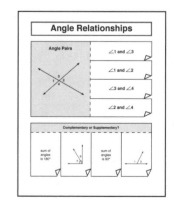

Angle Relationships

Angle Pairs

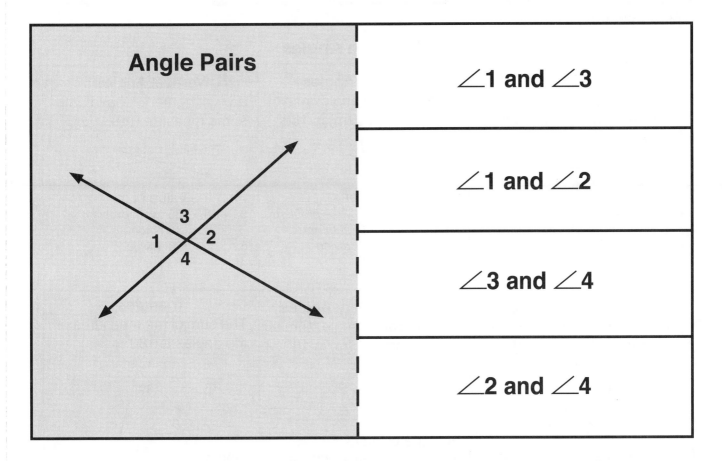

∠1 and ∠3

∠1 and ∠2

∠3 and ∠4

∠2 and ∠4

Complementary or Supplementary?

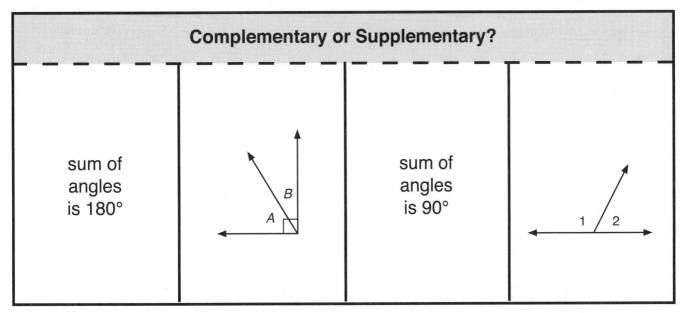

sum of angles is 180°

sum of angles is 90°

Student Instructions: Calculating Angles

Read the following information. Cut out the mini-lesson and attach it to the right-hand page of your interactive notebook. Use what you have learned to create the left-hand page.

✂

Mini-Lesson

Calculating Angles

Straight Angles
look like a straight line; the measure (m) of a straight angle is 180°.

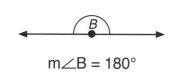

$$m\angle B = 180°$$

Adjacent Angles
form a straight angle; sum of their measures (m) is 180°.

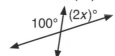
100° (2x)°

Find the value of x.
100 + 2x = 180 *write problem*
-100   = -100 *subtract*
          $\frac{2x}{2}$ = $\frac{80}{2}$ *divide*
          x = 40

Vertical Angles
are congruent; have the same measure (m).

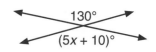
130°
(5x + 10)°

Find the value of x.
5x + 10 = 130 *write problem*
    - 10 = -10 *subtract*
$\frac{5x}{5}$ = $\frac{120}{5}$ *divide*
    x = 24

Complementary Angles
form a right angle; sum of their measures (m) is 90°.

64°
x

Find the value of x.
64 + x = 90 *write problem*
-64   = -64 *subtract*
    x = 26

Supplementary Angles
form a straight angle, sum of their measures (m) is 180°.

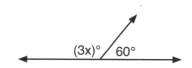
(3x)° 60°

Find the value of x.
3x + 60 = 180° *write problem*
    -60 = -60 *subtract*
$\frac{3x}{3}$ = $\frac{120}{3}$ *divide*
    x = 40

Triangles
The sum of the measures of the angles is 180°.

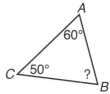
A
60°
C 50°   ? B

Find m∠B.
m∠B + 50 + 60 = 180° *problem*
m∠B +   110   = 180 *simplify*
        -110 = -110 *subtract*
        m∠B = 70°

Create Your Left-Hand Notebook Page

Step 1: Cut out the title and glue it to the top of the notebook page.

Step 2: Cut out the *Vertical and Adjacent Angles* flap book. Cut on the solid line to create two flaps. Apply glue to the back of the gray tab and attach it below the title. Under each flap, find the value of x. Show your work.

Step 3: Cut out the *Complementary and Supplementary Angles* flap book. Cut on the solid line to create two flaps. Apply glue to the back of the gray tab and attach it below the *Vertical and Adjacent Angles* flap book. Under each flap, find the value of x. Show your work.

Step 4: Cut out the *Find m∠C* flap piece. Apply glue to the back of the gray tab and attach it at the bottom of the page. Under the flap, find m∠C. Show your work.

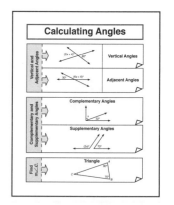

Calculating Angles

Vertical and Adjacent Angles

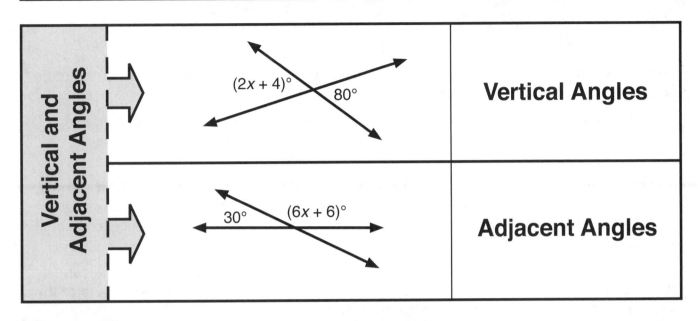

Vertical Angles

Adjacent Angles

Complementary and Supplementary Angles

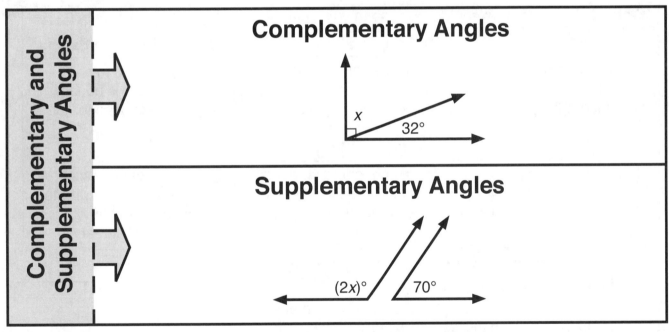

Complementary Angles

Supplementary Angles

Find m∠C.

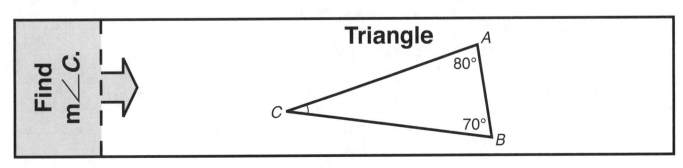

Triangle

Student Instructions: Surveys

Read the following information. Cut out the mini-lesson and attach it to the right-hand page of your interactive notebook. Use what you have learned to create the left-hand page.

Mini-Lesson

Surveys

Statistics is the study of data (information). A **statistical question** is used to gather data about a group. The group being studied is called the **population**.

Example: How many books do middle-school students read in one month?

Population: middle-school students
Data being studied: number of books read in one month

A **survey** is a tool used to collect statistical data. Only part of the population, called a **sample**, is surveyed. Not all samples are good or valid. A **valid sampling** accurately represents the population being studied. This type of survey allows you to correctly draw a conclusion about the population.

There are two types of sample surveys: biased and unbiased. **Unbiased** samples accurately represent the entire population being studied. In **biased** samples, one or more parts of the population receive greater representation than others.

Statical Question: How many books do middle-school students read in one month?		
Type of Sample	**Method**	**Biased/Unbiased Sample**
<u>Random Sample</u>: Members of the survey are randomly chosen.	All middle-school students' names were placed in a box. Without looking, the principal drew one hundred names.	<u>Unbiased</u>: Each middle-school student is equally likely to be chosen for the survey.
<u>Convenience Sample</u>: Members of the survey are chosen because they are easily accessible.	The first hundred students entering the school library were selected.	<u>Biased</u>: Students visiting the library received greater representation than other middle-school students.

Create Your Left-Hand Notebook Page

Step 1: Cut out the title and glue it to the top of the notebook page.

Step 2: Fill in the blank on the *Definition* piece. Cut out the piece. Apply glue to the back and attach it below the title.

Step 3: Fill in the blank on the *Survey* flap book. Cut out the book. Cut on the solid lines to create three flaps. Apply glue to the back of the gray tab and attach it below the title. Under each flap, write the definition.

Step 4: Complete the two *Sample Survey* flap pieces. Cut out the pieces. Apply glue to the back of each gray tab and attach them at the bottom of the page. Under each flap, justify your answer.

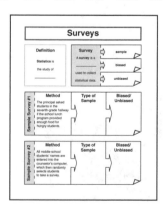

Surveys

Definition

Statistics is

the study of

_____.

Survey

A **survey** is a

_____

used to collect

statistical data.

→ sample

→ biased

→ unbiased

Sample Survey #1

Method	Type of Sample	Biased/ Unbiased
The principal asked students in the seventh-grade hallway if the school lunch program provided enough food for hungry students.		

Sample Survey #2

Method	Type of Sample	Biased/ Unbiased
All middle-school students' names are entered into the counselor's computer, which then randomly selects students to take a survey.		

Student Instructions: Measures of Center & Variability

Read the following information. Cut out the mini-lesson and attach it to the right-hand page of your interactive notebook. Use what you have learned to create the left-hand page.

Mini-Lesson

Measures of Center & Variability

Measures of center and variability are used to compare data.

A **measure of center** is a single number that describes the center of a set of data.

The **mean** is the average of a group of numbers. It is found by first finding the sum of all the values in the set of numbers. Then divide the sum by the total number of values in the set. **Example:** 2, 3, 5, 7, 9, 10 $$2 + 3 + 5 + 7 + 9 + 10 = 36$$ $$36 \div 6 = 6$$ Therefore, 6 is the mean.	The **median** is the number that is in the exact middle of the data set. Odd number of values: middle number. 7 is the median. **Example 1:** 2, 5, 6, **7**, 8, 9, 11 Even number of values: average of two middle numbers **Example 2:** 4, 5, 7, **8**, **9**, 12, 14, 16 Therefore, 8.5 is the median.

The **mode** is the number in a data set that occurs most often. **Example:** 2, 5, 6, 7, 8, 8, 9 Therefore, 8 is the mode. (Some data sets may not have a mode.)

A **measure of variability** is a single number that describes the spread of a set of data.

Range is the difference between the greatest and least values in the set of data.
    Example: **20**, 34, 43, 64, **91**   So, $91 - 20 = $ **71**. Therefore, the range is 71.

Interquartile Range (IQR) is the distance between the first and third quartiles of the set of data. **Example:** 9, 10, 13, 19, 20, 25, 29 **Step 1:** Find the median. Place parentheses around the numbers above and below the median. This makes Q1 and Q3 easier to identify. (9, 10, 13), **19**, (20, 25, 29) **Step 2:** Find the median for both Q1 and Q3. (9, **10**, 13), 19, (20, **25**, 29) Q1 = 10 and Q3 = 25. **Step 3:** Subtract Q1 from Q3. $25 - 10 = $ **15**. Therefore, 15 is the interquartile range.	**Mean Absolute Deviation (MAD)** is the average difference between each value and the mean in a set of data. **Example:** 65, 85, 80, 70. **Step 1:** Find the mean. Mean is 75. $65 + 70 + 80 + 85 = 300$ $300 \div 4 = 75$ **Step 2:** Subtract each value and the mean. $75 - 65 = $ **10**; $75 - 70 = $ **5**; $80 - 75 = $ **5**; $85 - 75 = $ **10** **Step 3:** Add all values. $10 + 5 + 5 + 10 = $ **30** **Step 4:** Divide sum by the number of values. $30 \div 4 = 7.5$ or $7\frac{1}{2}$ Therefore, 7.5 is the mean absolute deviation.

Create Your Left-Hand Notebook Page

Step 1: Cut out the title and glue it to the top of the notebook page.

Step 2: Cut out the *Data Set* flap piece. Attach it by the gray tab in the space below the title. Under the flap, write the numbers in the data set in numerical order.

Step 3: Cut out the *What's the difference?* flap book. Attach it by the gray center tab at the bottom of the page. Write the definitions under the flaps.

Step 4: Use the ordered data set to complete the *Finding Measures of Center and Measures of Variability* chart. Show your work. Cut out the chart. Apply glue to the back and attach it at the bottom of the page.

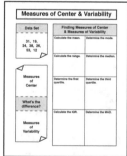

Measures of Center & Variability

Data Set
31, 19, 24, 38, 26, 53, 12

Measures of Center
What's the difference?
Measures of Variability

Finding Measures of Center & Measures of Variability

Calculate the mean.	Determine the mode.
Calculate the range.	Determine the median.
Determine the first quartile.	Determine the third quartile.
Calculate the IQR.	Determine the MAD.

Student Instructions: Comparing Data Sets

Read the following information. Cut out the mini-lesson and attach it to the right-hand page of your interactive notebook. Use what you have learned to create the left-hand page.

Mini-Lesson

Comparing Data Sets

The measures of center and measures of variability for numerical data from random samples can be used to draw inferences about a population. Graphs can be used to show the distribution of the data. The **distribution** is described by its shape. If the left side of the data distribution looks like the right side, then the distribution is **symmetric**.

Graphs Showing Symmetrical Distribution

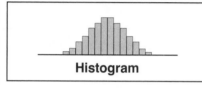

Histogram

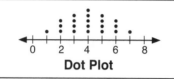

Dot Plot

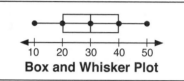

Box and Whisker Plot

The shape of the distribution can help you choose which measure is best to use to describe the center and variability (spread) of the data.

Type of Distribution	Measure of Center	Measure of Variability
both sets of data are symmetric	mean	mean absolute deviation
neither set of data is symmetric	median	interquartile range
one set of data is symmetrical	median	interquartile range

Example: <u>Statistical question</u>: How many times have you used social media this month?

Math Class 1

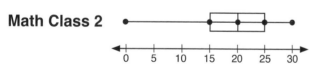

Math Class 2

Neither box is symmetric. Use the median to compare the centers and the interquartile range to compare the variations.

	Math Class 1	Math Class 2
Median	10	20
IQR	20 – 5 = 15	25 – 15 = 10

<u>General Inference</u>: Math Class 2 used social media more than Math Class 1.
<u>Measure of Center Inference</u>: The median for Math Class 2 is twice the median for Class 1.
<u>Measure of Variability Inference</u>: There is a greater spread of data around the median for Math Class 1 than for Math Class 2. Class 1 has a spread of 15.

Create Your Left-Hand Notebook Page

Step 1: Cut out the title and glue it to the top of the notebook page.

Step 2: Fill in the blanks on the *Data Distribution* piece. Apply glue to the back and attach it below the title.

Step 3: Cut out the graph flap book. Cut on the solid lines to create three flaps. Apply glue to the top section and attach it at the bottom of the page. Under each flap, write the answer.

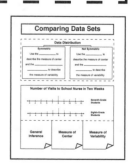

Comparing Data Sets

Data Distribution

Symmetric	Not Symmetric
Use the _____ to describe the measure of center and the _____ _____ _____ to describe the measure of variability.	Use the _____ to describe the measure of center and the _____ _____ to describe the measure of variability.

Number of Visits to School Nurse in Two Weeks

Seventh-Grade Students

Eighth-Grade Students

General Inference	Measure of Center	Measure of Variability

Student Instructions: Probability

Read the following information. Cut out the mini-lesson and attach it to the right-hand page of your interactive notebook. Use what you have learned to create the left-hand page.

Mini-Lesson

Probability

Probability is the chance or likelihood that an event will happen. The result of an event happening is called an **outcome**. Outcomes occur at **random** if each outcome is equally likely to occur. The probability of an event occurring can be described with a ratio. Since any ratio can be converted into a fraction, decimal, or percent, you can also convert any probability into a fraction, decimal, or percent.

$$\text{P(likelihood an event will occur)} = \frac{\text{number of favorable outcomes}}{\text{number of possible outcomes}}$$

Example:	Event	$\dfrac{\text{number of favorable outcomes}}{\text{number of possible outcomes}}$	Probability
Rolling a die with sides numbered 1 through 6.	rolling a 3 P(3)	$\dfrac{\text{only one 3 on the dice}}{\text{six equally likely outcomes}}$	$\dfrac{1}{6}$ $P(3) = \dfrac{1}{6}$

The probability of an event is represented as a number between 0 and 1. The probability of 0 means that the event will never occur. A probability of 1 means the event will always occur. Any fraction or decimal between 0 and 1 tells you how likely the event is to occur. The closer to 0, the less likely an event will occur. The closer to 1, the more likely an event will occur. A number line can be used to show the likelihood that a particular outcome will happen.

	Impossible (will never happen)	Unlikely	Even Chance	Likely	Certain (will always happen)
Fraction	0	$\frac{1}{4}$	$\frac{1}{2}$	$\frac{3}{4}$	1
Decimal	0	0.25	0.5	0.75	1
Percent	0%	25%	50%	75%	100%

Create Your Left-Hand Notebook Page

Step 1: Cut out the title and glue it to the top of the notebook page.

Step 2: Find the probability of a coin toss coming up heads. Write the answer as a fraction, percent, and decimal on the *Heads or Tails* puzzle piece. Cut out the puzzle piece. Apply glue to the back and attach it below the title.

Step 3: Cut out the *Unlikely or Likely* flap puzzle piece. Attach by the gray tab below the *Heads or Tails* puzzle piece. For each given probability, explain whether it means that the event is unlikely or likely to occur. Write the answers under the flap.

Step 4: Cut out the *Marbles* puzzle piece. Apply glue to the back of the top section and attach at the bottom of the page. Under the flap, explain each statement.

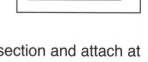

Probability

Heads or Tails

P(h)

Fraction: _____

Decimal: _____

Percent: _____

Unlikely or Likely

The probability that the spinner will land on green is $\frac{8}{9}$.

The probability that Donna will win the game is $\frac{1}{4}$.

Marbles

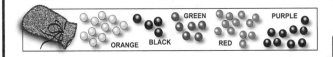

Number of Marbles

There are 42 marbles in the bag. The marble colors are orange, black, green, red, and purple.

Certain

If you draw a marble from the bag, it is certain that the marble color will be orange, black, green, red, or purple.

Impossible

If you draw a marble from the bag, it is impossible for the color to be brown.

Student Instructions: Uniform Probability Model

Read the following information. Cut out the mini-lesson and attach it to the right-hand page of your interactive notebook. Use what you have learned to create the left-hand page.

Mini-Lesson

Uniform Probability Model

Probability is a measure of the likelihood that an event will happen. The set of all the possible outcomes is called the **sample space (S)**. In a **uniform probability model**, each outcome has an equal probability of happening. In a **non-uniform probability model**, each outcome has a different chance of occurring.

Uniform Probability Model—One Flip of the Coin

S = {head, tail} (Outcomes)	$\dfrac{\text{possible outcome}}{\text{total possible outcomes}}$	Probability
		$P(h) = \frac{1}{2}$
		$P(t) = \frac{1}{2}$

Non-uniform Probability Model—One Draw From Jar

S = {square, triangle} (Outcomes)	$\dfrac{\text{possible outcome}}{\text{total possible outcomes}}$	Probability
		$P(\text{square}) = \frac{3}{5}$
		$P(\text{triangle}) = \frac{2}{5}$

Create Your Left-Hand Notebook Page

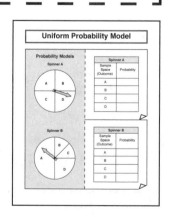

Step 1: Cut out the title and glue it to the top of the notebook page.

Step 2: The spinner for each model on the *Probability Models* flap book is spun one time. Fill in each table with the possible outcomes. Cut out the flap book. Cut on the solid line to create two flaps. Apply glue to the back of the gray left-hand section and attach it below the title.

Step 3: Under each flap, tell if the model has uniform probability. Explain your answer.

Uniform Probability Model

Probability Models

Spinner A

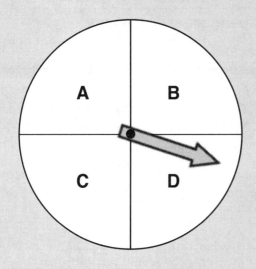

Spinner A	
Sample Space (Outcome)	Probability
A	
B	
C	
D	

Spinner B

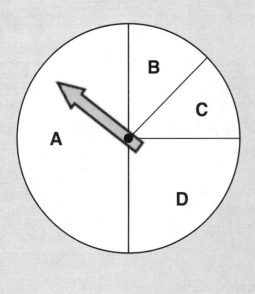

Spinner B	
Sample Space (Outcome)	Probability
A	
B	
C	
D	

Student Instructions: Theoretical & Experimental Probability

Read the following information. Cut out the mini-lesson and attach it to the right-hand page of your interactive notebook. Use what you have learned to create the left-hand page.

Mini-Lesson

Theoretical & Experimental Probability

Probability is a measure of the likelihood that an event will happen. There are two types of probability: theoretical and experimental. Both probabilities are ratios that compare the number of favorable outcomes to the total number of possible outcomes.

Theoretical probability:	Experimental probability:
$P(\text{event}) = \dfrac{\text{number of favorable outcomes}}{\text{total number of possible outcomes}}$	$P(\text{event}) = \dfrac{\text{number of times event occurs}}{\text{total number of trials}}$

Compare Theoretical and Experimental Probability

Theoretical probability is what we expect to happen during a probability experiment.

> **Example:** Imagine that you tossed a coin 10 times. You would expect to get heads one-half the time or 5 times out of 10. Since there are only two outcomes, you have a 50/50 chance of getting heads.

Event: P(h)	$\dfrac{\text{number of favorable outcomes}}{\text{number of possible outcomes}}$	Probability
tossing heads	$\dfrac{5}{10}$	$P(h) = \dfrac{1}{2}$

Experimental probability is what actually happens during a probability experiment.

> **Example:** Your team tosses a coin 10 times. The table shows the experimental probability. The coin landed on heads 6 times out of 10.
>
> Experimental probability: $P(e) = \dfrac{\text{number of times event occurs}}{\text{total number of trials}}$
>
> $P(h) = \dfrac{6}{10}$ or $\dfrac{3}{5}$

Trials	
Outcomes	**Frequency**
Heads	6
Tails	4
Total	10

Compare Probabilities

The two measures of probability of an event may or may not be the same. As the number of attempts increase, the theoretical and the experimental probability should become closer in value.

$\dfrac{1}{2} \approx \dfrac{3}{5}$ The theoretical probability is close to the experimental probability. If they had not been close, one possible explanation is there were not enough trials.

Create Your Left-Hand Notebook Page

Step 1: Cut out the title and glue it to the top of the notebook page.

Step 2: Cut out the *Deck of 16 Cards* piece. Apply glue to the back and attach it below the title.

Step 3: Answer the questions on the *Probability* flap piece. Apply glue to the back of the top section. Attach the piece at the bottom of the page.

Step 4: Under the flap, compare the experimental probability of selecting a heart to its theoretical probability.

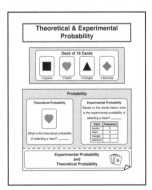

Theoretical & Experimental Probability

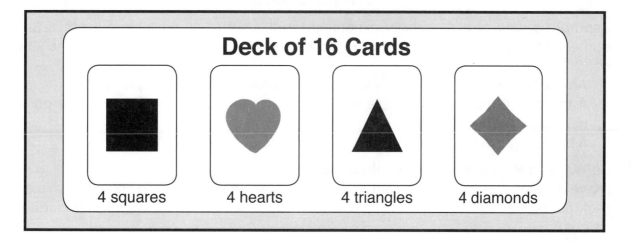

Deck of 16 Cards

| 4 squares | 4 hearts | 4 triangles | 4 diamonds |

Probability

Theoretical Probability

What is the theoretical probability of selecting a heart? _____

Experimental Probability

Based on the results below, what is the experimental probability of selecting a heart? _____

Card	Frequency
square	2
heart	6
triangle	3
diamond	5

Experimental Probability and Theoretical Probability

Student Instructions: Sample Space

Read the following information. Cut out the mini-lesson and attach it to the right-hand page of your interactive notebook. Use what you have learned to create the left-hand page.

Mini-Lesson

Sample Space

The **sample space** of a probability experiment is the set of all possible outcomes for the experiment. Organized lists, tables, and tree diagrams are three ways to represent the sample space.

- An **organized list** contains all the possible outcomes for the sample space.
- A **table of outcomes** is a table where the rows and columns represent the possible outcomes in each event.
- A **tree diagram** is a drawing representing the total possible outcome.

Three Ways to Represent the Sample Space

You have a black shirt (BS), a red shirt (RS), and a green shirt (GS), and you also have a pair of black pants (BP) and a pair of tan pants (TP). Possible outcomes or possible number of outfits are 6.

Organized List of the Sample Space: BB, BT, RB, RT, GB, GT

Table of Outcomes

Shirts	Black Pants	Tan Pants
black shirt	black shirt black pants	black shirt tan pants
red shirt	red shirt black pants	red shirt tan pants
green shirt	green shirt black pants	green shirt tan pants

Tree Diagram

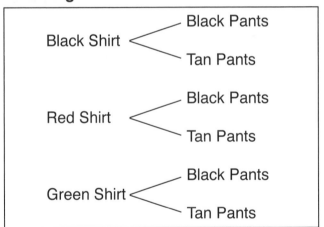

Create Your Left-Hand Notebook Page

Step 1: Cut out the title and glue it to the top of the notebook page.

Step 2: Cut out the *Situation* piece. Apply glue to the back and attach it below the title.

Step 3: Complete the *Table of Outcomes* piece. Cut out the piece. Apply glue to the back and attach it below the title.

Step 4: Cut out the *Organized List of Outcomes* flap piece. Apply glue to the back of the gray tab and attach it at the bottom of the page. Under the flap, write the sample list.

Step 5: Complete the *Tree Diagram* piece. Cut out the piece. Apply glue to the back and attach it at the bottom of the page.

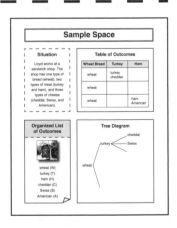

Sample Space

Situation

Lloyd works at a sandwich shop. The shop has one type of bread (wheat), two types of meat (turkey and ham), and three types of cheese (cheddar, Swiss, and American).

Table of Outcomes

Wheat Bread	Turkey	Ham
wheat	turkey cheddar	
wheat		
wheat		ham American

Organized List of Outcomes

wheat (W)

turkey (T)

ham (H)

cheddar (C)

Swiss (S)

American (A)

Tree Diagram

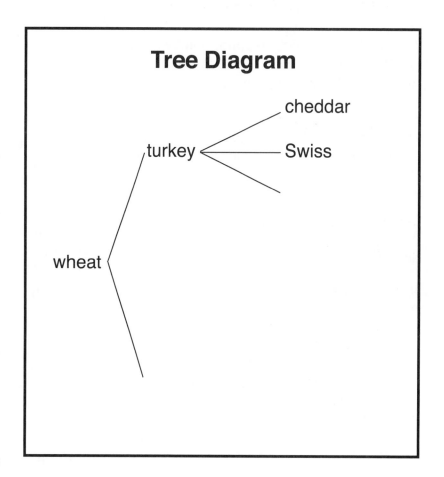

Answer Keys

Answers are limited to those not presented as part of the mini-lessons on each "Student Instructions" page.

Integers & Absolute Value (p. 5)

What is the Opposite?: 1. -5 2. 6
Absolute Value (clockwise from top) $|-8| = 8$,
$|-13| = 13$, $|9| = 9$, $|3| = 3$

Adding & Subtracting Integers (p. 7)

Adding and Subtracting Integers Rules:
Rule 1: piece #2 Rule 2: pieces #1, #5
Rule 3: pieces #3, #4

Adding & Subtracting Using Mathematical Properties (p. 9)

Commutative Property of Addition: Card C
Associative Property of Addition: Card E
Identity Property of Addition and Subtraction: Card A
Additive Inverse Property: Card B
Addition and Subtraction Inverse Properties: Card D

Working With Rational Numbers (p. 11)

$\frac{1}{12} = 0.08\overline{3}$ repeating, $\frac{4}{5} = 0.8$ terminating,
$\frac{3}{8} = 0.375$ terminating, $\frac{7}{12} = 0.58\overline{3}$ repeating

Adding & Subtracting Rational Numbers (p. 13)

Which Tip?: (clockwise from top) front flaps:
$-23\frac{1}{10}$, $11\frac{1}{12}$, 61.62, 1.63, 39.565, -14.25

Multiplying Fractions & Mixed Numbers (p. 15)

Multiply a Fraction by a Fraction: Steps: multiply the numerators/multiply the denominators and simplify;
$\frac{3}{16}$
Multiply a Fraction by a Whole Number: Steps: rewrite, multiply, and simplify; $7\frac{3}{4}$
Multiply a Mixed Number: Steps: rewrite, multiply, and simplify; $16\frac{2}{3}$

Multiplying & Dividing Using Mathematical Properties (p. 17)

1. zero product property
2. inverse property of multiplication and division
3. commutative property of multiplication
4. associative property of multiplication
5. identity property of division
6. distributive property

Multiplying & Dividing Integers (p. 19)

1. 65 2. 313 3. -12 4. -1,323
5. -8 6. 468 7. 21 8. 4,539
Rule 1: 1, 2, 6, 7, 8   Rule 2: 3, 4, 5

Unit Rates & Fractions (p. 21)

Step 1: Rewrite fraction horizontally as a division problem. $8\frac{1}{2} \div \frac{3}{4}$
Step 2: Rewrite the problem using the reciprocal.
$\frac{17}{2} \div \frac{4}{3}$
Step 3: Solve the problem by multiplying and simplifying. $\frac{17}{2} \times \frac{4}{3} = 11\frac{1}{3}$

Proportional Relationships (p. 23)

Is the Relationship Proportional?: Yes, Yes;
the cross products are equal.
Walking Trip:

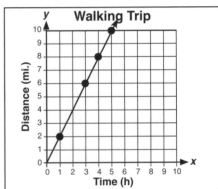

Constant of Proportionality (p. 25)

What is the Constant?: Graph constant: 0.5
Table constant: 45

Using Variables (p. 27)

Phrases and Expressions: (Letters used for variables may vary.) $3x - 8$, $2(9 \div x)$, $y + 52$, $20 \div (3t)$
Evaluating Expressions: $17t + 7 = 75$,
$\frac{35}{x} + 9y = 70$

Mathematical Properties & Equivalent Expressions (p. 29)

1. $34 \cdot 64$, commutative property of multiplication
2. $4 \cdot 9 - 4 \cdot 6$, distributive property
3. $1 \cdot 35 = 35$, identity property of multiplication
4. $8 + (5 + 2)$, associative property of addition
5. $23 \cdot (6 \cdot 5)$, associative property of multiplication
6. $6 \cdot 13 + 6 \cdot 27$, distributive property

Solving Two-Step Equations (p. 31)

$$3g + 5 = 35$$
$$\underline{\quad -5 \quad -5 \quad}$$
$$3g \quad = 30$$

$$\frac{3g}{3} = \frac{30}{3}$$
$$g \quad = 10$$

$$6m - 12 = 13$$
$$\underline{\quad +12 \quad +12 \quad}$$
$$6m \quad = 25$$

$$\frac{6m}{6} = \frac{25}{6}$$
$$m \quad = 4.166$$

$$\frac{c}{2} + 5 = 7$$
$$\underline{\quad -5 = -5 \quad}$$
$$\frac{c}{2} \quad = 2$$

$$2 \cdot \frac{c}{2} = 2 \cdot 2$$
$$c \quad = 4$$

$$3z - 2 = 10$$
$$\underline{\quad +2 \quad +2 \quad}$$
$$3z \quad = 12$$

$$\frac{3z}{3} = \frac{12}{3}$$
$$z \quad = 4$$

Two-Step Inequalities (p. 33)

$$4x - 7 < 5$$
$$\underline{\quad +7 \quad +7 \quad}$$
$$4x \quad < 12$$

$$\frac{4x}{4} < \frac{12}{4}$$
$$x \quad < 3$$

$$-9x + 2 \leq -16$$
$$\underline{\quad -2 \quad -2 \quad}$$
$$-9x \quad \leq -18$$

$$\frac{-9x}{-9} \leq \frac{-18}{-9}$$
$$x \quad \geq 2$$

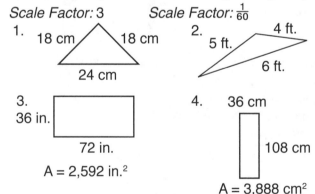

Scale Drawings of Geometric Figures (p. 35)

Scale Factor: 3
1.
18 cm   18 cm
24 cm

Scale Factor: $\frac{1}{60}$
2.
4 ft.
5 ft.
6 ft.

3.
36 in.
72 in.
A = 2,592 in.²

4.
36 cm
108 cm
A = 3,888 cm²

Three-Dimensional Figures (p. 37)

Rectangular Prism: 8 vertices, 12 edges, 6 faces, rectangle shape
Cone: 1 vertex, 0 edges, 1 face, triangle shape
Square Pyramid: 5 vertices, 8 edges, 5 faces, square shape

Circumference (p. 39)

Diameter: 23.864 m   *Radius:* 100.48 ft.
Diameter: 12.56 in.   *Radius:* 42.704 m

Area of a Circle (p.41)

(Clockwise from top): 379.94 ft.², 452.16 cm², 78.5 m², 254.34 in.²

Angle Relationships (p. 43)

Angle Pairs (top to bottom): adjacent, vertical, vertical, adjacent
Complementary or Supplementary (left to right): supplementary, complementary, complementary, supplementary

Calculating Angles (p. 45)

Vertical Angle:
$$2x + 4 = 80$$
$$\underline{\quad -4 = -4 \quad}$$
$$\frac{2x}{2} = \frac{76}{2}$$
$$x = 38$$

Adjacent Angle:
$$30 + 6x + 6 = 180$$
$$36 + 6x \quad = 180$$
$$-36 \quad = \quad -36$$
$$\frac{6x}{6} = \frac{144}{6}$$
$$x = 24$$

Complementary Angle:
$$x + 32 = 90$$
$$\underline{\quad -32 = -32 \quad}$$
$$x \quad = 58$$

Supplementary Angle:
$$2x + 70 = 180$$
$$\underline{\quad -70 = -70 \quad}$$
$$\frac{2x}{2} = \frac{110}{2}$$
$$x = 55$$

Triangle:
$$m\angle C + 80 + 70 = 180°$$
$$m\angle C + 150 = 180$$
$$\underline{\quad -150 = -150 \quad}$$
$$m\angle C = 30°$$

Surveys (p. 47)

Sample Survey #1: convenience, biased, The lunch program is for all middle-school students, but only part of the population, seventh grade, was surveyed.
Sample Survey #2: random, unbiased, Each middle-school student is equally likely to be chosen for the survey.

Measures of Center & Variability (p. 49)

Mean: 12 + 19 + 24 + 26 + 31 + 38 + 53 = 203 ÷ 7 = 29
Mode: No mode   *Range:* 53 − 12 = 41
Median: 26   *First quartile:* 19
Third quartile: 38
IQR: 19
   Step 1: 12, 19, 24, **26**, 31, 38, 53
   Step 2: (12, **19**, 24), 26, (31, **38**, 53)

Step 3: Q1 = **19** and Q3 = **38**

Step 4: 38 − 19 = **19**, IQR = **19**

MAD: 10

Step 1: $\dfrac{12 + 19 + 24 + 26 + 31 + 38 + 53}{7}$ = **29**

Step 2: 29 − 12 = **17**, 29 − 19 = **10**, 29 − 24 = **5**, 29 − 26 = **3**, 31 − 29 = **2**, 38 − 29 = **9**, 53 − 29 = **24**

Step 3: 17 + 10 + 5 + 3 + 2 + 9 + 24 = **70**

Step 4: $\dfrac{70}{7}$ = **10**

Comparing Data Sets (p. 51)

Data Distribution:
Symmetric – mean, mean absolute deviation
Not Symmetric–median, interquartile range
General Inference: The average number of visits to the school nurse was the same for both classes.
Measure of Center: The median for both grades is 8.
Hint: Even number of values in the data set, so median is the average of the middle two values.
seventh-grade data set:
5, 7, 8, 8, **8**, **8**, 9, 10, 11, 11; $\dfrac{8 + 8}{2}$ = **8**

eighth-grade data set:
6, 7, 7, 8, **8**, **8**, 8, 9, 9, 10; $\dfrac{8 + 8}{2}$ = **8**

Measure of Variability: The interquatrile range for both grades is 2.
Hint: Find median of Q1 and Q3. Subtract Q1 and Q3.
Seventh-Grade:
(5, 7, **8**, 8, 8) (8, 9, **10**, 11, 11,); 10 − 8 = **2**
     Q1   Q3
Eighth-Grade:
(6, 7, **7**, 8, 8,) (8, 8, **9**, 9, 10); 9 − 7 = **2**
     Q1   Q3

Probability (p. 53)

Heads or Tails: Fraction: $\frac{1}{2}$, Decimal: 0.5, Percent: 50%
Unlikely or Likely: Green–Likely, probability is closer to 1 than 0.
Donna wins–Unlikely, probability is closer to 0 than 1
Marbles: Certain–The marble colors are orange, black, green, red, and purple. Therefore, if you draw a marble from the bag, it is certain that the marble color will be orange, black, green, red, or purple. Impossible–There are no brown marbles. Therefore, if you draw a marble from the bag, it is impossible for the color to be brown.

Uniform Probability Model (p. 55)

Spinner A:
Spinner A is a uniform probability model. Each outcome has probability of $\frac{1}{4}$.

Spinner A	
Sample Space (Outcome)	Probability
A	$\frac{1}{4}$
B	$\frac{1}{4}$
C	$\frac{1}{4}$
D	$\frac{1}{4}$

Spinner B:
Spinner B is a non-uniform probability model. Each outcome does not have the same chance of occurring.

Spinner B	
Sample Space (Outcome)	Probability
A	$\frac{1}{2}$
B	$\frac{1}{8}$
C	$\frac{1}{8}$
D	$\frac{1}{4}$

Theoretical & Experimental Probability (p. 57)

Theoretical Probability: $\frac{4}{16}$ or $\frac{1}{4}$

Experimental Probability: $\frac{6}{16}$ or $\frac{3}{8}$

Experimental Probability and Theoretical Probability: The theoretical probability is $\frac{1}{4}$ and the experimental probability is $\frac{3}{8}$. The two probabilities are not close. One possible explanation: there were not enough trials.

Sample Space (p. 59)

Organized List of Outcomes: WTC, WTS, WTA, WHC, WHS, WHA
Table of Outcomes: turkey/Swiss, turkey/American, ham/cheddar, ham/Swiss
Tree Diagram:

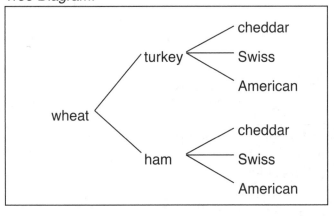